W9-CXO-700

READER PRAISE FOR MANAGE I.T.

"This easy to read, practical book bridges the gap between management and technology skills. Reading Manage I.T. and applying the principles it contains will make you a better manager and help you add more value to your organization. I highly recommend it."

KEN BLANCHARD, CO-AUTHOR THE ONE MINUTE MANAGER

"Manage I.T. is a valuable reference of actionable insights and instructions for IT leaders. Clearly explaining both fundamentals and complexities, Santana and Donovan present examples and resources illustrating how to maximize leadership skills and avoid blunders that can ruin an IT career. From mistakes made in hiring; to a guide for determining how much of the IT budget should be invested in running, growing or transforming the company's business; to advice on how to benefit you and your IT team if your company decides to outsource your function, it's a guidebook no IT manager should miss reading."

PETER BENDOR-SAMUEL, CHIEF EXECUTIVE OFFICER, EVEREST GROUP, AUTHOR, TURNING LEAD INTO GOLD:THE DEMYSTIFICATION OF OUTSOURCING

"A must read for budding IT managers. The authors are painstakingly careful to offer a step-by-step self-testing process that goes well beyond simply examining whether to make the leap into management. Throughout they probe and exhort the reader to be very clear on satisfying both personal and professional outcomes before making that move. The authors offer sensible cases and situations that also benefit from an uncommonly inviting writing style for the subject matter."

DR. DONALD J. CALISTA, DIRECTOR GRADUATE CENTER FOR PUBLIC POLICY MARIST COLLEGE

"New I.T. managers will get a lot of value out of this book. It's packed with practical guidance from the real-world experiences of Joe and Jim and the best part is that this guidance can be deployed immediately."

DR. JON COUTURE, SENIOR VICE PRESIDENT HR SIEMENS BUSINESS SERVICES, INC

"One of the most frequent problems I have encountered in my 25 years of leadership and learning work within a variety of organizations is the botched transition from expert employee to manager of others. Manage I.T. by Joe Santana and Jim Donovan hits the nail on the head. Their book with plain speaking and rich examples outlines how the problem occurs and what senior execs and managers can do to make the situation a win for everyone. I can't imagine an IT professional who would not gain from reading this book."

T.J. ELLIOT, CHIEF LEARNING OFFICER ETS, PRINCETON, N.J.

"This is clearly a landmark book in that it is really the first to fully integrate notions of IT value with the IT workplace at the group and individual level. People have talked about the role of "people" in achieving business and IT results. This book makes the tie-in from end to end like no other book has. Simply outstanding."

DR. HOWARD A. RUBIN, MEMBER OF THE BOARD
AND EVP META GROUP, INC

"Every IT manager and would-be-IT manager should read this book and learn how to prevent blunders that are costly to their company and to their personal career. Those targeting the next level will find this book an excellent tool for giving themselves an IT career health-check."

JOSEPH SABRIN, EVP AND FOUNDER eHire.com
(FORMER FOUNDER AND PRESIDENT OF DATA EXECUTIVES, PC
ETCETERA, AND MANTECH COMPUTER SERVICES, INC.)

"Manage I.T. is a mentoring book that will help both business managers who need to understand technology and technology managers who need to understand business.Ê Santana and Donovan have created a much needed reality-based management workbook. Manage I.T. is self-help at its best — full of totally pragmatic advice and illustrated with real world business nuggets."

PRISCILLA TATE, FOUNDER AND EXECUTIVE DIRECTOR,
TECHNOLOGY MANAGERS FORUM

MANAGE
I.T.

MANAGE
I.T.

A Step-by-Step Guide to Help New and
Aspiring IT Managers Make the Right
Career Choices and Gain the Skills
Necessary for Peak Performance

JOE SANTANA & JIM DONOVAN

L̦P

LAHASKA PUBLISHING
BUCKINGHAM, PENNSYLVANIA

LAHASKA PUBLISHING
POST OFFICE BOX 1147
BUCKINGHAM, PA 18912

www.lahaskapublishing.com

ISBN: 0-96505349–0

Library of Congress Control Number: 2002110945

Thanks to Dr. Jon Couture, Senior Vice President Human Resources, Siemens Business Services, for permission to use his Employee Lifecycle Model© in chapter 9. The materials are reprinted with permission, and are copyright ©1997 Dr. Jon Couture. All rights reserved

Copyright © 2002 by Joe Santana and Jim Donovan

All rights reserved. No part of this book may be reproduced or transmitted in any form or by any means, electronic or mechanical, including photocopying, recording or by any information storage and retrieval system, without permission in writing from the publisher.

Printed in the United States of America

TABLE OF CONTENTS

ACKNOWLEDGEMENTS

First and foremost, I would like to thank my co-author Jim Donovan, whose incredible experience as a published author of several successful books and as a book coach provided me with invaluable guidance and direction. Without Jim, I don,t think this book would have been completed.

My next heartfelt thanks go to Peter Bendor-Samuel, Jon Couture, Howard Rubin, Joseph Sabrin and Pricilla Tate for their contributions of ideas and thought leadership. I appreciate the time each of these seminal thinkers carved out of their busy schedules to share their unique perspectives and insights.

I also want to thank, the renowned Ken Blanchard and our other pre-publication readers, which include, Donald Calista and T.J. Elliot for taking the time from their busy schedules to read the manuscript and supply their illuminating comments.

Finally, I want to thank all of my friends and family for their patience with my weekends of work, late evenings of writing and the prolonged exits from personal activities that it took to work on this book. Of this group, a special extra thanks goes out to Lizzy for being my personal organizer, Ken for taking the time to read and provide feedback on the early manuscript and Eileen for supplying input on style and her general support and encouragement.

Joe Santana

Special thanks to my friend of many years and co-author, Joe Santana, for bringing this opportunity to me and for his incredible commitment to making it the best it could be. Joe, you *are* amazing. Thanks to everyone at Lahaska Publishing for their dedication to excellence, especially Christina Rivas, Megan Nodwell, Donna Eliassen, and Joel Powell for their editorial and design assistance. Thanks to Maria Bentley for her creative publicity help and to my wife and best friend, Georgia for her love, patience and support.

Jim Donovan

FOREWORD

This is a practical, easy to use, book that will help your career and bring you greater happiness and balance in your life, while increasing the value you add to your company. We will start you on your personal journey by sharing our many years of experience and expertise to guide you first, with a look inside yourself to see if a career in IT management is the right choice for you. Then, if you decide that IT management is right for you, read on and we will show you, in simple and straight-forward language, how you can acquire the key skills you need to get on the fast-track to peak performance.

For example, you will learn:

- To use simple models to gain focus, perspective and direction in your new role as a manager and leader of a team.
- To seize as opportunities, and gain benefits for yourself and your team, from changes in the IT space that have disrupted others.
- Where to go to get up-to-date, specialized information so you can continue to develop your new skills and remain on the leading edge in the I.T. space.

If you are currently trying to decide if you should accept an IT management position, read this book before you decide. If you are a new IT manager, read this book and get a fast start. If you are a "seasoned" IT manager, read this book and become a better one. If you are helping someone decide whether they should become an IT manager and/or helping them transition into the role of an IT manager, read this book with them and use it as the basis for training and coaching them through the process.

We highly recommend reading and rereading this book and completing the exercises because it is packed with information that you can put to use immediately and continue to use throughout your entire IT management career.

Joe Santana and Jim Donovan

INTRODUCTION

Learning is not compulsory... neither is survival.

W. Edwards Deming

This book was written for newly promoted IT managers or candidates considering the leap into management. Our purpose is to help you determine whether going into IT management is the right choice for you, and if you decide that it is, to give you a basic grounding in the new skill set and mindset that you will need to achieve peak performance in your new career.

According to a major study, every year American companies lose $350 billion due to having disengaged employees (The Gallup Management Journal Online Columns). The primary reason for these employees being disengaged is the lack of management and leadership ability among the ranks of their direct managers. Nowhere is this problem of weak management ability more painful and prevalent than in Information Technology.

The key reason for this is that the skills of an IT manager are so different from those of an IT practitioner (which we sometimes refer to as a doer) that experience and success in the latter do not prepare one or indicate ability for success in the former. Furthermore, the entire process of promoting new IT managers from the ranks of IT professionals is, at best, weak, even among some of the most enlightened organizations. Many companies will simply "anoint" the new IT manager and expect him/her to "learn the ropes." "She was a great programmer, so she will be a great IT manager," you often hear. And so, every year, thousands of companies promote star technical performers into IT management roles, with high expectations that they will automatically "figure out what to do" and love their new bigger-title job. What will happen in most cases, however, is easily predictable. As they move through this unguided promotion process into the role of IT manager, many formerly confidant and stellar workers will become less-than-stellar managers.

These new and unhappy IT managers will then repeat the classic blunders of their equally unguided predecessors, and rack up a sizable portion of that $350 billion per year expense. Given the huge importance of IT alignment and the necessity for strong leadership in order for a company to successfully execute its strategic plans, the true impact most likely exceeds even this hefty price tag. Worse still, the individuals who left their successful positions as high-quality technology performers to become poor-performing managers also suffer in terms of personal confidence, happiness, and in some cases, the derailing of what otherwise could have been a successful non-managerial career.

The good news is that if you have been recently offered a promotion to IT management or are a potential candidate for a management position, there is a great deal you can do to keep your career on track.

Avoid having your promotion become a career disaster

There are two very important things that you can do to avoid career disaster. First and foremost, make sure that IT management is the right move for you. Moving from a role as a technical professional to a role as the manager of technical professionals is a big decision. It will place a huge demand on you to learn new ways of working and thinking. If your core values and needs are not satisfied by the demands and rewards of an IT management position, we can guarantee that you will not be successful and that you will become progressively more unhappy.

Secondly, if you decide that IT management is the right career move for you, approach it with the understanding that even though you are working for the same company, you are, in effect, starting a new job. You will no longer be the top technician, but rather an entry-level manager. Your new job will require new skills as well as a new mindset. Be open, prepared to learn, and prepared to abandon your old role completely.

Experts in Human Capital Management today are rapidly recognizing that the model of assessing an employee's need for orientation, coaching, support, learning, and development, based on how long the person has been with the company, tends to fall short. Under this old model, your need for orientation was thought to end upon the completion of a ninety-day career with the company.

After that, you were a member of the team who knew his/her way around. If you were promoted to a new role a year later, you were expected to simply hit the ground running, like a pro. Today, we know that this is not how it works.

Recent models recognize that an employee's need for orientation, coaching, support, learning, and development are cyclical, and that the commencement of a new "lifecycle" is triggered by a role change. One of these models, the Employee Lifecycle© HR Model, was developed in 1997 by Dr. Jon Couture, a Senior Vice President of Human Resources with a global technology consulting and outsourcing company. In Dr. Couture's model, an employee lifecycle represents the time, from beginning to end, that an employee spends in a specific role within the company. For example, if you have been promoted twice, and moved laterally once, over a period of six years, you are considered to have enjoyed three lifecycles in a six-year career with your employer. Dr. Couture points out that every role change places the employee at the beginning of a new lifecycle.

The proof of the value of this cyclical, systematic approach to supporting people can be seen in the success of businesses who have successfully used this model as a means of promoting and supporting a highly mobile workforce of knowledge-workers in a manner that has improved employee productivity and satisfaction, while reducing employee turnover to a level below the industry standard. This model embodies one of the most important methods employed by the company in becoming the employer of choice in the IT consulting and outsourcing space. It is a huge plus in an industry fueled by knowledge-workers.

How this book will help you

This book will help you in two ways. It will provide you with step-by-step guidance in making an honest self-assessment that will assist you in deciding if the IT management role being offered is the right career move for you. For those of you who decide it is the right move, we will provide you with the basic foundation you need to get a solid start toward becoming a peak performer. Here, then, is a brief chapter by chapter overview.

The *first chapter* of this book is designed to help you to make a well thought-out career decision. We do this by providing you with specific examples designed to help you get a better understanding of the IT management role, as well as helping you take into consideration some of the pros and cons of the specific job offer you are considering. If, after going through the exercises in chapter one, your conclusion is, "No, I don't think I want to do this," then put this book down and read no further. Go to whomever offered you the promotion, thank them for their confidence, and then graciously decline. Assuming, however, that your answer is, "Yes, this job is for me," the balance of this book will help you develop a strong foundation toward your success.

In the *second chapter*, we will help you to develop a chart that will enable you to begin orienting yourself to your new position. This chart will let you see and validate assumptions about the relationship between your company's big picture strategy and the work you and your team are charged with performing.

Chapters three through six will give you a basic grounding in some of the most useful skills you will need to learn to be effective as a new IT manager. Please note that this by no means represents everything you need to learn to be an effective IT manager. It is simply a collection of some of the most common things that you will most likely need to learn. Consider this a starting, not ending, point in your development as a new IT manager.

The *seventh chapter* will walk you through the process of doing something that is often harder than acquiring new skills and practices—letting go of old practices and tasks. This "shedding" skill is important, because unless you master it quickly, you will never be able to focus your time and energy on the things that will enable you to produce the most value in your new role as an IT manager. You will also block the creativity and productivity of your people.

The *eighth chapter* will give you a brief overview of a growing force in the IT space, which you may encounter as an IT manager—outsourcing. Today, more and more companies are outsourcing large and small components of IT. Your resistance can be harmful to your company, and it will, in time, bring your career growth to a halt. In this chapter, we will show you how to take a fresh look at actions that will help both you and your company benefit from outsourcing.

Chapter nine is a bonus offering. It presents a complete reprint of Dr. Couture's Employee Lifecycle© HR Model white paper. Those of you who are interested in working with your HR departments to implement a cyclical approach to supporting your team members will find this chapter of great value.

Finally, at the end of this book, you will find a list of resources you can use to continue to build on the foundation you will establish using this book. We strongly urge you to use these as a starting point, and to continue to build upon them for the rest of your career.

In summary, in addition to helping you decide if IT management is right for you, this book will provide you with the tools you need to quickly orient and socialize yourself into your new role (one of the most important components of success, and yet one of the most frequently skipped steps of Couture's lifecycle model).

"Learning," as Dr. Edwards Deming once said, "is not compulsory." Right now, no one is driving or pushing you to read this book. The choice is yours. The information it contains, however, can make a huge difference to your surviving and even thriving in your IT career. In addition to providing you with the authors' combined forty-six years of experience drawn from the world of IT Management and Human Development, you will receive insights from some of the best experts in the field. Experts whose insights and perspectives will affect your ability to successfully execute the role of an IT manager.

We are grateful for the opportunity to lead you through this exciting journey to career success. So let's begin by making sure that IT management is the right choice for you!

1

DO YOU REALLY WANT TO DO THIS?

Make your life a mission — not an intermission.

ARNOLD GLASGOW

While this chapter title may seem funny, our goal is not to amuse you; it is to drive home the importance of the question. We are all familiar with movies or plays built around the classic theme of "the road not taken." A few of the works elegantly portraying this subject include If by Lord Dunsany (1921), It's A Wonderful Life by Frank Capra (1946), and the more recent Sliding Doors by British actor Peter Howitt. The plot in each of these basically shows us how a future state of unhappiness or happiness is determined by a single choice that sets the direction for everything else that follows. If you examine the life of anyone—from the corporate executive to the prison inmate—you will see that, somewhere along the way, a definitive choice was made.

Most organizations today select their new IT management candidates from among their top performers. This seems like a logical and intelligent way to do things. They basically take someone who has proven his/her value in one area and give him/her more responsibility. So why does it so often fail?

One reason is that the new IT manager lacks some of the basic orientation and skills needed to be an effective manager and leader. The bulk of this book is designed to fill those gaps.

There is, however, another reason for failure; that IT management might not be the "right road" for some people. It is the purpose of this chapter to help you assess yourself, so you can decide if IT management is the right choice for you before you commit any additional time and effort to moving in that direction. Specifically, we want to make sure you choose the right road for you, before you embark on too long of a journey.

Joe — Having been in IT for over two decades, I've seen my share of people in the wrong roles, and I have come to recognize the telltale signs. For example, some years ago, I joined an IT service supplier company as the head of a unit handling a number of infrastructure support processes for a major client. One thing I always do when I accept a new management assignment is to get to know all the people on the team reporting directly or indirectly to me. That's how I met Jack (not his real name). Jack was a newly promoted supervisor who had been a top performer as a team member, but was now, according to his manager, a terrible manager.

I met with Jack, and after gaining his confidence, got him to share with me how he really felt about his management role. In a nutshell, he hated it, but feared that if he stepped down he would appear a failure to his peers and his team. It was clear to me that IT management was not the right choice for him. We devised a plan that allowed him to gracefully move back into the technical field as a contributor, without appearing to have been demoted. The end result was that Jack became a dynamic contributor again, and since then has gotten a number of promotions along the technical track to a very well paying and challenging position that he undoubtedly enjoys.

Perhaps you have already started on the journey we speak of. You've already accepted a promotion to IT management and now find yourself "not having fun." If that is the case, we recommend that you do not skip this chapter and jump straight into the next sections of this book, thinking, "Oh well, I've already made my choice, so let me just push ahead."

We believe that if IT management turns out not to be the right choice for you, you, your organization, and your current team will all benefit more from your "back-tracking" away from IT management, instead of trying to "push on" when every fiber of your being is pulling you in another direction.

To make an intelligent assessment of your personal compatibility with the role of IT manager, you first need to have a better picture of the IT manager's role. Let's take a closer look at what IT managers do.

What does an IT manager do?

So, what does an IT manager do, and how does that differ from what an IT practitioner ("doer") does? We did an exercise not too long ago, in which we looked at a group of people who were in the IT space and determined what their specific skillsets were. Here's a brief overview of some of the specific skills for the IT practitioner (doer) in the area of repair and customization of hardware, compared with the skills of the person who manages the doers.

The doer:

- Installs and customizes software.
- Installs and fixes printers.
- Assists in the set-up of network services.
- Replaces parts in machines.
- Repairs malfunctioning software.

The manager of that person:

- Monitors and directs the daily activities of the team.
- Provides guidance and support to the team, and reconciles activity reports that show the productivity of the team.
- Continually seeks ways to improve the quality of the service.
- Continually seeks ways to reduce the cost of the service.
- Directs and navigates the team through various changes necessitated by changes in the business.
- Makes sure the right capacity and coverage of people is in place, based on the needs of the business.
- Builds the knowledge and skills of the team so that they are in alignment with the needs of the company.

Very different types of jobs, right? Your specific technical job and IT manager role or target role may be slightly different. Nevertheless, they will be just as different from each other as the ones in the above example, because all technical positions are "direct contributor" oriented, whereas management roles have a large "indirect" component.

The point here is very clear. While becoming an IT manager may seem like a natural progression from serving as an IT professional, they are actually two very different types of positions, built upon different skills and competencies.

How does the manager role differ from the doer role?

One of the most knowledgeable and well-rounded IT professionals in the business today is Priscilla Tate, the founder and Executive Director of the New York-based Technology Managers Forum. Tate tells us that "technology professionals are similar to baseball players, whereas IT managers need to be coaches." Tate tells us that she is not surprised by the high failure rate of successful IT performers dropped into management roles. "It simply is a totally different job, where the technical knowledge becomes context and the key value-generating skills are non-technical," she states.

Usually, coaches are former baseball players who know the game well. However, as coaches, their focus is on drawing out the best baseball skills from their players. To do this, they employ their personal talents for nurturing, communicating, and motivating others; the common elements in all good managers. The same holds true for the best IT managers. The former "technical components" of their jobs as technology professionals become context, just like the former baseball playing skills of the coach. The table below contains a side-by-side view of some of the generic skills and competencies employed by a technology professional, and those employed by good IT managers at a high level. A quick look at this table brings home the full impact of Tate's message in comparing team members to baseball players and managers to the coach.

TECHNOLOGY PROFESSIONAL	IT MANAGER
Skills Employed • Technical subject knowledge • Problem-solving skills • Knowledgeable user of technology hardware and/or software tools (e.g. diagnostics)	**Skills Employed** • Understanding and maintaining team alignment with the bigger company and IT picture • Communication • Motivating people and drawing out the best in them • Setting goals and direction • Giving feedback • Helping team members to further develop their skills and capabilities • Delegating work to the right team members

What motivates good IT managers?

Good IT managers not only use a different set of skills than their team members, they also have a different set of what we call "personal behavior drivers." For example, great managers are likely to:

- Focus on understanding their people and their innate strengths.

- They are curious about people and generally ask people questions in order to understand them and their motivations.

- Enjoy creating heroes rather than being the hero.

- See themselves more as a coach than as a teacher. The subtle difference is that teachers input content into people, whereas coaches bring out the best that already resides within their charges. (Although managers may still do some teaching.)

- Be sensitive to what each person in their charge needs in order to do their best (e.g., a moment of distraction, or to be given room to quietly focus their thoughts).

- Be cultivators who carefully water and prune their "garden of people," with deep respect for the land.
- Have a highly developed sense of empathy that gives them insight into other people.

In short, a good IT manager is generally someone who is capable, willing, and enjoys being "the wind beneath someone else's wings."

Profiling the IT Manager Role

Below is a generic profile of the talents, gifts, and personal propensities of a good IT manager, based on the information we've discussed so far in this chapter.

Generic IT Manager Role Drivers — Primary Talents/Gifts/Mindset Profile.

What does an IT manager need to be able to do easily?

Communicate with senior managers, peers, and their team members.

Bring out the best performance from individuals and teams.

Guide, support, and direct team members as needed, without over-managing them.

What do good IT managers generally love to do that makes them feel rewarded by this role?

Coach and support the performance of others.

Develop the skills, talents, and capabilities of other people.

Plan and orchestrate results that bring success to their teams.

What tend to be some of the goals of people who are successful in this role?

To be "star-makers" (as opposed to "stars").

To be great communicators.

To display and inspire confidence.

What do good IT managers generally do naturally, almost automatically?

Get to know their people.

Learn and stay in touch with the big picture in their company and field.

Break down and explain things.

Do you fit the basic IT manager profile?

The following are profiles of three different people considering a move into IT management. As you read through these, look for similarities between yourself and the people profiled.

Mary is a top-notch IT technician and a star performer on her team. She is happy in her work and enjoys the many accolades she receives for her accomplishments. Mary enjoys the variety of projects she has the opportunity to work on within the company. She's always working on one or two new ideas to help drive improvement and has a few "pet" projects. If you asked her what she likes most about her job, she would say, without the slightest hesitation, that she likes "the limelight," solving problems, and seeing immediate results.

Fred is a hardware whiz. He is willing to help his co-workers, but he gets a little restless and annoyed when he has to share his knowledge of hardware and technology with people who don't quickly "get it." He does, however, enjoy talking about the latest gadgets and technology with peers who match his expertise. On weekends, Fred likes to "tinker" with his computer at home, adding components and software tools. Fred is the kind of person who likes things done quickly and feels that few people can do his job as quickly or as well as he can. If you asked Fred what he likes most about his job, he would say tinkering, solving problems, learning more about new technology, and getting work done with his own hands.

Elizabeth is one of the top IT software developers in her company. While Elizabeth is a star individual performer, she's also the first one to step forward when someone else needs help in learning how to solve a problem. Although she's very talented in her own right, she has always enjoyed nurturing others and helping them discover how to tap into their own pool of talents to solve problems. She's also a great organizer and volunteers to take the lead for special projects whenever the opportunity arises. "Liz (Elizabeth) just makes me feel secure, like I really know what I'm doing and my contributions count," explains Jim, a young developer Elizabeth has "unofficially" taken under her wing. Elizabeth simply has a knack for bringing out the best in the people she works with, and she enjoys doing it. While Elizabeth has enjoyed being a software developer, she's become aware over the last two years that her personal focus has evolved into more enjoyment of teaching, coaching, and organizing others to success. If you asked her what she currently enjoys most about her job, she would point to the projects where she had an opportunity to orchestrate a team of people to success. She is especially proud of the progress made by Jim.

Do you see yourself in any of these people? If you are more of an Elizabeth, the chances are that you are pretty well suited for the move into IT management. Elizabeth exhibited some of the key traits and values of a good manager. She is a nurturer, a star maker. This does not mean that Mary or Fred might not become good managers. But if, like Mary and Fred, you enjoy being the technical expert, the "go-to-person," and "the star," chances are you won't want to give up the enjoyment you get out of your current role in order to make someone else the expert, the go-to-person, and the star.

One more final question: Are you willing to pay the price?

So, let's say that on reading the examples above, you conclude that your personality and career focus are well-suited to IT management. Good, now we need to make sure that you are willing and able to accept any additional challenges or cons that this new position may bring. For example, in your company as an IT manager, you may be required to travel more and to be out of town for longer periods of time. Or perhaps you will be asked to relocate or attend weekend meetings every month. You may not consider some of the things listed here as "cons." Or perhaps they are "mild cons." The important thing that we want you to do is to think about all of the items that you might consider cons, and factor these in along with the pros when making your decision. This is part of what we call being willing to "price your pay" for accepting this role.

In making this decision, we think you will find useful a simple pro and con exercise used by Benjamin Franklin when he was faced with an important choice. Here is how you can set up your own pro and con decision-making table:

On a piece of paper, draw a table with two columns.

- Label the first column *Pros.*
- Label the second column *Cons.*
- List all of the benefits of accepting the IT management position in your company in the *Pros* column.
- List all of the negative cost factors of accepting the IT management position in your company in the *Cons* column.

Using the Elizabeth profile above, let's see how this works. Suppose that Elizabeth, after determining that she would enjoy the role of IT manager, collected information on the specifics of this new job and the results were as follows:

- Attend 7 a.m. meetings with my boss regularly.
- Stop working on the "mCommerce Genesis Project."
- Meet with vendors/suppliers each week to go over work performance.
- Work with more people and develop teams.
- Opportunities to coach and help people grow.
- Significant increase in salary.

- Fast-track my career.
- Achievement and recognition from higher-ups in the company.
- Relocate five hundred miles away from my current location.
- Travel an additional sixty days per year.

Based on her current life situation and other factors, Elizabeth views some of these items as pros and others as cons. (You may consider them differently). Here is her Pro/Con Decision-Making Table.

PRO'S	CON'S
• Meet with vendors/suppliers each week to go over work performance. • Work with more people and develop teams. • Opportunities to coach and help people grow. • Significant increase in salary. • Fast-track my career. • Achievement and recognition from higher-ups in the company.	• Attend 7 A.M. meetings with my boss regularly. • Stop working on the "mCommerce Genesis Project." • Relocate five hundred miles away from my current location. • Travel an additional sixty days per year.

Elizabeth's Pro/Con Decision-Making Table

Looking at the cons, Elizabeth realizes that they will not have a major negative impact on her. She usually gets to the office at 8 a.m., but actually works at home from 6:20 a.m. to 7:20 a.m. She will need to get to the office earlier on the meeting days, but her wake-up time will be the same. She likes the "Genesis Project," but she is more thrilled by the prospect of heading up a team, so she's okay with giving that up. The relocation is a bit tougher and so is the travel, but given the benefits offered by the pro column items, she decides to accept the position.

The point here is that there are clearly some big and little cons, but after consciously weighing them, an uncluttered and positive decision resulted. This is much better than accepting the job, letting these things "float up" later, and feeling miserable. What is most important is not the complete absence of cons, but rather your decision after honestly looking at all the pros and cons.

Always make sure you stay happy the "Warren Buffett way"

When speaking to a group of students at the University of Nebraska, Warren Buffett, one of the richest men in the world, said, to the surprise of his audience, "I am really no different from any of you. If there is any difference between you and me, it may simply be that I get up every day and have a chance to do what I love to do—every day. If you want to learn anything from me, this is the best advice I can give you."

ACTION ITEMS:

1: Think and determine if you fit the general profile of someone who is a "star-maker, communicator, nurturer, and coach." (If you like sports, ask yourself who you admire and model yourself against most, a coach like John Wooden or one of the players.)

2: List the specific things that will change if you accept this IT management position, and then compare the pros and cons using the Benjamin Franklin Pro / Con Decision-Making Table.

3: Decide to accept or decline.

If your decision is to not accept this position because the work does not appeal to you, then stop reading right here and consider how much time, energy, and pain you saved yourself and others by reading just these few pages.

If your decision is to not accept this position because, while the work does appeal to you, the cons for this specific job outweigh the pros, then either read to prepare for the next opportunity or tuck this book away until the time comes when you need it.

If your decision is to accept the position because the work appeals to you and the pros outweigh the cons, then please proceed immediately to the next chapter, where we will begin your orientation into this new exciting role with an introduction to the foundation-setting topic of alignment. We will tell you what it is, why it is important for you to understand it, how you can create it, and how you can maintain it.

2

ACHIEVING ALIGNMENT FOR YOURSELF AND YOUR TEAM

A rock pile ceases to be a rock pile the moment a single man contemplates it, bearing within him the image of a cathedral.

ANTOINE DE SAINT-EXUPERY

Why is your understanding of alignment important?

Alignment of IT with the business is one of the oldest topics in Information Technology. It refers to how closely an organization's IT strategy is interwoven with, supports, and drives its overall business strategy. For example, if a company is in a business that requires a great deal of research and development, and the IT organization has a strong focus on developing and implementing technologies to support collaboration and the collection of knowledge needed for the research, then this IT organization is well-aligned with the company's strategy. On the other hand, if IT is spending the bulk of its time, budget, and effort on supporting a word-processing application used by the administrative arm of the company, we would have to say that it is poorly aligned with the company's strategy. Understanding how IT is aligned with the business, and what role you play in supporting and maintaining that alignment, is the key to enabling you to "see the big picture."

As a team's manager and leader, one of the things your people will expect from you is direction and guidance. In order to do this, you need to see, understand, and communicate the shape and direction of that ever-changing big picture. It is imperative that you see this "big picture," and never lose sight of it, in order to make sure that your personal efforts, as well as the efforts of your team, support your organization. The best way to obtain and maintain your own personal alignment, as well as the alignment of your team, with the company strategy or big picture is to chart your key objectives, back through IT, to the company strategy.

To get a better understanding of how this works, let's consider an example of two management positions in the same company. One new manager has been appointed to run the IT Help Desk, and the other will run the Client Relationship Management Application Development and Support Group. Let's further assume that the company's strategy is as follows:

- To grow their rate of profitability from their current clients by 10%.

- To expand their overall share of the market for their products and services by 2%.
- To expand their presence from the current national borders to the larger global market for their products and services.

Now, let's look at how these company objectives will shape the overall IT strategy, as well as the focus of the two IT departments, and ultimately, the jobs of the two new managers.

Company Objectives	IT Strategy	Help Desk Strategy	Help Desk Actions	Managers Actions
•Grow profitability from existing clients •Grow market share 2% each quarter •Expand into the global market from the current national presence	•Reduce transaction processing costs •Develop Client Relationship Management support solutions •Partner with a global eCommerce provider	•Provide an acceptable level of service quality •Manage and reduce costs •Give higher priority to issues affecting parts of the company that generate market share growth	•Use the Help Desk support application to segment high-and low-priority calls •Stagger shifts to avoid overtime •*Et Cetera*	•Identify and secure a consultant to work on customizing the Help Desk support application •Cross- train all agents, so they can cover any shift •*Et Cetera*

The New Help Desk Managers Alignment Chart

Company Objectives	IT Strategy	CRM Team Strategy	CRM Team Actions	Managers Actions
• Grow profitability from existing clients • Grow market share 2% each quarter • Expand into the global market from the current national presence	• Reduce transaction processing costs. • Develop Client Relationship Management support solutions • Partner with a global eCommerce provider	• Invest in developing superior CRM tools for the field • Establish a strategic partnership with a global sales pipeline management company	• Review options and implement new tools • Review short list of potential partners; select and contract a primary and a backup supplier • Train field on use of new tools	• Identify and select project team leaders • Facilitate the development of tool and supplier search criteria • Provide future field trainers with training on how to train

The New CRM Application and Support Manager's Alignment Chart

Looking at these two charts, you will notice that while the overall IT strategy remains the same, the department-level strategy and action plans are different. The reason for this is that each of these departments or teams supports the IT/business strategy in a different way. These differences will affect the manager's action plan focus. The Help Desk supports the IT/business strategy by providing support services at the lowest possible cost. In the case of the CRM team, because it is one of the key areas directly supporting the company strategy, its actions are geared toward making the most intelligent investments of people, time, and money.

In the above examples, we provided all of the key information about company strategy and IT alignment. Some of you reading this may not know your company's strategy and/or how IT is aligned with it. So, as a new manager, you may wonder—How can I develop this type of chart for myself and my new team? Helping you to do so is the focus of this chapter.

How to create your team and personal "Alignment Chart" using seven easy steps

There are seven steps you must take in order to create your own team and personal alignment chart. They are:

1. Find out your company's strategy.
2. Determine how IT is aligned with the business.
3. Determine where your team fits into the picture.
4. Draft the team's strategy and action plan.
5. Draft your personal action plan.
6. Review the team's and your personal action plan with your manager.
7. Finalize and communicate the plan to everyone.

Let's take a look at some of the tools, models, and resources you can use to execute these steps.

1. Find out your company's business strategy

With the exception of some non-profit organizations, companies are economic entities that focus on increasing their value and the wealth of their owners by meeting the needs of a market. Where they differ is in the specifics of how they expect to achieve this goal. The method via which they plan to achieve their goal is called the company's strategy.

For some companies, the strategy is to derive more revenue from an existing client base. For others, it's to increase the profitability of their existing business and revenue. And for still others, it's to extend the company into a new line of business. The potential list is as endless as our imagination.

Fortunately, companies do not keep their strategies secret. In fact, they regularly communicate their strategies to the public though a number of channels. One of these is the company's annual report. If your company generates an annual report, you will find the strategy clearly spelled out in the President's or CEO's letter that summarizes the previous year's activity and lays out the plan for the following year.

Here are just a few of the places where you can obtain information on your company's strategy:

Your company's website, under "Information for Investors" and "Press Kits."

www.hoovers.com

www.business.com

Look for the answers to the following two questions, and you will find that they sum up the company's basic objective and high-level plan for reaching that objective.

What is the most important thing that the company is focused on achieving?

What are the top two or three ways that the company intends to reach its objective?

Your company, for example, may be focused on becoming more

profitable by increasing the margins drawn out of current contracts and expanding the overall number of contracts. You can then drill down to specific metrics and you will have the information needed to fill out the first column of your chart.

2. Use the IT Investment Portfolio Model to determine how IT is aligned with your company's business

One of the biggest struggles that business and IT executives have faced over the years is establishing a common language that enables them to discuss IT relative to business strategy requirements. In recent times, that search has resulted in ITs co-opting the language of investment portfolio management as a means of communicating the alignment between IT and the objectives of the business. "The use of the Investment Portfolio Model in conversations between IT and the business provides a form of universal translator between two alien species, namely business and IT people," stated Howard Rubin, META Group EVP and founder of the Metricnet website.

Rubin, who has been leading the charge to adopt portfolio management models in IT as a means of creating a clear language, tells us that using this model enables everyone in IT to understand their role relative to supporting the business strategy. We agree, and believe that by giving you a small tutorial in the IT Investment Portfolio Model, we will not only help you see the big picture, but this will also give you a tool for staying in sync with that picture whenever it changes.

The chart below shows the layers of the Portfolio Model as explained by Rubin and indicates who is responsible for managing each layer.

Portfolio Model Component	Contents	Managers/Owners
The overall IT investment fund	The entire IT budget allocated by the company for IT expenses and investments.	Jointly owned by the Chief Information Officer (or whoever heads up IT) and the chief Financial Officer.
A Portfolio	A collection of products and services that are similar in nature. For example, the distributed computing services.	The VP or direct report of the CIO who is responsible for the delivery of these services.
A product or service	A single unit of value or investment within a portfolio. For example, in distributed computing, the Help Desk is a single unit.	The manager of the unit.

In Rubin's model, all IT investments will fit into one of three major portfolios. The chart below identifies each portfolio, its contents, the risk/reward factors inherent in the particular component, and the decision-making factors (drivers).

Portfolio	Contents	Risk/Reward/ Decision Drives
Run - the - Business Portfolio	IT investments in products and services that do not directly help the company differentiate itself, drive revenue, or change the business. They are, however, basic commodities needed by the company to be in business. (For example, a break/fix operation.)	Risks/Rewards • Low risks and low rewards Decision-Making Drivers • Par Quality is okay • Cost containment and savings
Grow - the - Business Portfolio	IT investments in products and services that directly affect the generation of revenue and/or profitability out of the current business model. (For example, a CRM application.)	Risks/Rewards • Mid risks and mid rewards Decision-Making Drivers • Par to excellent quality needed • Return on investment (ROI)
Transform - the - Business Portfolio	IT investments in products and services that do not affect the generation of revenue and/or profitability out of the current business model, but instead change the business into a new model or way of doing business. (For example, R&D dollars spent on developing a new mBusiness or mCommerce business model.)	Risks/Rewards • High risks and high rewards Decision-Making Drivers • Par to excellent quality needed • Probability estimates

Let's take a close look at each of the three IT portfolio categories.

Run-the-Business

This portfolio contains IT investments that are basic commodities needed by the company to be in business. These are investments that do not directly help the company differentiate itself in a manner that drives revenue growth, increases profitability, or effects change in the business. There are some items that generally go in this category in almost every instance, such as break/fix services. The real determining factor, however, of what will be placed into this category is the role that a particular IT product or service plays within a company. So, as a rule, anything that does not clearly go into the Grow-the-Business or Transform-the-Business categories, but that needs to be done to remain in business, belongs here.

Due to the low impact that Run-the-Business items have on the business, they are generally low risk and low reward items. Most companies do not want to be sub-par in these services, but there isn't a benefit to investing a lot of money to excel in these areas. As a matter of practice, most businesses will invest enough to have a par level of service (good, but not great), and will focus on reducing costs in this space.

Grow-the-Business

These are IT investments that directly support the generation of revenue and/or profitability out of the current business model. Again, there are some types of IT services and products that generally find their way into this fund, such as CRM applications, but as in the other categories, the key determining factor is the role a service plays within a specific business.

Due to the fact that the services and products in this portfolio have an effect on revenue, profitability, and market share, they offer higher risks and corresponding higher rewards to the company than investments in the Run-the-Business portfolio. Companies compare and choose between Grow-the-Business investment options using return on investment (ROI) analysis. Those services and/or products offering the highest ROI will be selected over other services and products.

Transform-the-Business

This category of IT investment includes investments that are made to change the business into a new model or way of doing business. For example, a company's investments toward creating a new mobile commerce retail model to replace a brick and mortar or eCommerce model is a Transform-the-Business investment.

Transform-the-Business investments hold the highest risks and promise the greatest rewards for a company. Since you are generally dealing with relatively new technologies and business models, you do not really know if your investments are being well-placed. Imagine a company in the early stages of the video player era, preparing a taped sales campaign to be distributed to all potential customers on the BetaMax™ format, based on the assumption that this format was going to become the standard.

On the other hand, if you do your homework, make the right "guesstimates," and keep your hand close enough to the pulse, you could end up being the first in your industry to corner a new model and the largest portions of the rewards. (Companies that are the first in a market generally enjoy an advantage which is sustained for a generous amount of time relative to the competitors that follow.) A good example of this is the Sony Walkman™.

How to use the model to secure your IT division's contribution to alignment

Now that we've taken a close look at the IT Investment Portfolio Model, let's see how it works in a few example scenarios. Please re-read what follows as many times as you need in order to fully understand and internalize it.

How an organization groups its IT services into the various portfolio categories (Run-the-Business, Grow-the-Business, and Transform-the-Business), and how it allocates the percentage of dollars invested into each portfolio is driven by the corporate strategy. Here are some examples:

Suppose we take the company in the example given earlier. Their stated objectives were to:

- Increase their rate of profitability from their current clients by 10%.

- Expand their overall share of the market for their products and services by 2%.

- Expand their presence from the current national borders to the larger global market for their products and services.

Now, let's say that the company is a software development company, and that they plan to achieve these goals by excelling in the creation of greater customer intimacy through world-class support. The Customer Support Center they use also doubles as their internal Help Desk. Their grouping of their IT services across portfolios might look like this:

Portfolio	Items Grouped in Portfolio	% of Budget Allocation Goals
Run-the -Business Portfolio	Break/fix, internal desk-side support, some hosted applica-tions, *et cetera*.	40%, with downward trend over the year until it reaches 35%.
Grow-the- business portfolio	CRM applications, customer support tools, customer-centric hosted applications, the Help Desk, *et cetera*.	50%
Transform-the-Business Portfolio	R&D on mSupport for mobile users (a small but growing segment of the client base.)	10%

The above tells you that this IT organization considers the Help Desk, which in many cases is considered a Run-the-Business item, as a Grow-the-Business item, because it is part of meeting a Grow-the-Business-focused plan. (The plan is to grow the business through world-class support, and this Help Desk supports the company's clients as well as their internal people.) We also see that this company is allocating the largest share of their IT budget to the Grow-the-Business portfolio, which is in alignment with their Grow-the-Business strategic focus.

Let's look at another example. Suppose we had another company with an identical set of objectives. This company, however, is in the retail business, and their approach to meeting their Grow-the-Business objectives is based on point-of-purchase loyalty strategies (for example, customer discount cards for volume purchases). In this company, the grouping of IT services across portfolios might look like this:

Portfolio	Items Grouped in Portfolio	% of Budget Allocation Goals
Run-the -Business Portfolio	The Help Desk, break/fix, internal deskside support, some hosted applications, *et cetera.*	40%, with a downward trend year over year until it reaches 35%
Grow-the Business Portfolio	CRM applications, customer support tools, customer-centric hosted applications, *et cetera.*	50%
Transform-the-Business Portfolio	R&D on mSupport for mobile users (a small, but growing segment of the client base.)	10%

Notice how the Help Desk moved from the Grow-the-Business category into the Run-the-Business category. The reason for this is that in the case of this particular company, the Help Desk is not part of the Grow-the-Business strategy (it is simply an internal support service). The budget allocations are the same, because as in the previous example, this company has a Grow-the-Business focus, and is, therefore, investing more in IT solutions that support their Grow-the-Business strategy.

Now, just to thoroughly ground you in this model, let's look at one more example. Suppose we look at another company that has the following stated objectives:

- Transform a brick & mortar retail operation to an mCommerce service.

- Establish a whole new market for this new service.

- Identify current clients who fit the new profile and bring them over to the new business model.

This company's grouping of IT services across portfolios might look like this:

Portfolio	Items Grouped in Portfolio	% of Budget Allocations Goals
Run-the Business Portfolio	The Help Desk/fix, internal deskside support, some hosted applications, *et cetera*.	40%, with a downward trend year over year until it reaches 35%
Grow-the-Business Portfolio	CRM application support, *et cetera*.	10%
Transform-the-Business Portfolio	R&D on mSupport for mobile users, development of and support for a 24/7 redundant infrastructure.	50%

The most important change to notice in this chart is the decrease in Grow-the-Business investments and the significant increase in Transform-the-Business investments. The application of IT investments is in alignment with this company's Transform-the-Business strategy.

Key Points

Here are the key points from this section:

- Alignment refers to having IT investments applied in a manner that supports the execution of the business strategy.
- The IT Investment Portfolio Model creates a shared language between IT and business management.
- Items are grouped into portfolios, based on how they fit into the business strategy framework.
- The percentage of IT dollars invested is driven by the main thrust of the company's strategy, which is either to grow its current business or to transform it.

Once an IT investment is grouped into a specific fund, the framework of how to manage that product or service is established on the basis of the risks, rewards, and drivers that govern items in that portfolio.

3. Determine where your team fits into the big picture

The value of the IT Investment Portfolio Model is that it gives you a framework for establishing the appropriate big-picture understanding of the area you are managing.

For example, if you have been promoted into a management position that is in charge of a function that falls into the Run-the-Business space, then you realize that one of your key decision drivers is going to be cost control. You will also, more than likely, be expected to provide good service, but not to require large investments to provide excellent service. Why? Because all of the items grouped in the Run-the-Business space are managed to decrease costs and just "keep the lights on."

If, on the other hand, you're running a business that is in the Grow-the-Business space, your management framework is built upon *Return On Investment* (ROI). So, if you have multiple applications and services to choose from, in which you can invest resources or people, you have to consider: "If I put a dollar into project X, will it produce more return on investment than if I put a dollar into project Y?" You will decide what projects to fund, back, and direct your people and resources toward based on which ones result in the best ROI. Also, your risks and rewards are higher than those of people managing a Run-the-Business investment.

If you are the new manager over an area grouped into the Transform-the-Business portfolio, then you know that your risks and rewards are even higher. If you are in a company that has a business strategy focused on transforming the business, you will be expected to provide excellence in this space. You are what Howard Rubin calls "a venture capitalist," and you need to employ sound judgment and have a close eye on the ball to minimize losses and maximize wins.

By viewing yourself as managing a product grouped within one of these portfolios, you anchor yourself and your new team to the key objectives. This enables you to make sure that your management and leadership efforts will have the greatest impact on your team and organization, relative to the big-picture.

4. Draft your team's strategy and action plan

It may seem odd that we are drafting the team's action plan before the manager's, but if you think about it, it makes perfect sense. Your role as a manager is to be a coach, supporter, enabler, developer, and link to the organization. The fact is that you cannot do any of those things until you know what you are coaching toward, supporting, enabling, developing for, or linking to. To a great degree, if you've applied what you've learned so far, you probably know what you are linking to. Now you just need to fill in the other key pieces of information.

From our early example of the "Alignment Chart," you should by now have obtained the information necessary to fill out columns one, two, and three, as shown in the example below, using the information from the sample company discussed at the beginning of this chapter.

1. Company Objectives	2. IT Strategy	3. Help Desk Strategy	4. Help Desk Actions	5. Managers Actions
• Grow profitability from existing clients • Grow market share 2% each quarter • Expand into the global market from the current national presence	• Reduce transaction processing costs • Develop Client Relationship Management support solutions • Partner with a global eCommerce provider	• Provide an acceptable level of service quality • Manage and reduce costs • Give higher priority to issues affecting parts of the company that generate market share growth		

Your task now is to identify the specific actions that the team will take in executing the strategy (in this example, the Help Desk). To prime your thinking muscles, ask yourself, "What does the team have to do to attain the goals of this strategy?"

Once you've completed this step, you will be in a position to think about the role you will play, as a manager and leader, in helping your team to succeed.

5. Draft your personal action plan

Continuing with our example, let's now assume that the list you come up with and add into column four looks like this:

1. Company Objectives	2. IT Strategy	3. Help Desk Strategy	4. Help Desk Actions	5. Managers Actions
• Grow profitability from existing clients • Grow market share 2% each quarter • Expand into the global market from the current national presence	• Reduce transaction processing costs • Develop Client Relationship Management support solutions • Partner with a global eCommerce provider	• Provide an acceptable level of service quality • Manage and reduce costs • Give higher priority to issues affecting parts of the company that generate market share growth	• Use the Help Desk support application to segment high-and low-priority calls • Stagger shifts to avoid overtime • *Et cetera*	

The items in the fourth column represent things that your team needs to do in order to accomplish the objectives of the strategy. Now you are in a position to complete the picture by adding your action items to column five. To generate your list, answer the following question: "What do I need to do to support and coach my team, and give them the tools that they need to do their best and be successful?"

Once you complete this step, you will have a first draft of a plan for running a team that supports the overall alignment of IT with the company's strategy.

6. Review the team and your personal action plan with your manager

Now you need to make sure that you have the acceptance and support of your manager for your "view of the world." Your final document should look like the chart below.

1. Company Objectives	2. IT Strategy	3. Help Desk Strategy	4. Help Desk Actions	5. Managers Actions
• Grow profitability from existing clients • Grow market share 2% each quarter • Expand into the global market from the current national presence	• Reduce transaction processing costs • Develop Client Relationship Management support solutions • Partner with a global eCommerce provider	• Provide an acceptable level of service quality • Manage and reduce costs • Give higher priority to issues affecting parts of the company that generate market share growth	• Use the Help Desk support application to segment high-and low-priority calls • Stagger shifts to avoid overtime • *Et cetera*	• Identify and secure a consultant to work on customizing Help Desk support application • Cross-train all agents, so they can cover any shift • *Et cetera*

Schedule an appointment with your manager to review this draft. Your conversation in this meeting can go like this:

"The purpose of this meeting is to make sure that my plans and the basis for my plans for managing my area are in support of the company's goals and your goals. In putting this draft together, I researched our company strategy, how IT supports that strategy, and specifically how my team and I support that strategy. The result is this Alignment Chart. I would like to make sure that it covers all of the right areas from your perspective."

From there, go into a column-by-column review of the chart, and note whatever changes and modifications develop from the meeting.

7. Finalize and communicate the plan

Once your manager has approved a final draft, get in front of your team and present this information. Get their feedback and input on specific ways of achieving certain goals. Communicate this plan frequently, and work key points into all of your written and oral communications. Do not assume that after that first meeting "everyone's got it." Consistent and regular communication of how the team contributes to the big picture is actually one of the ways in which you keep people engaged.

Maintaining your alignment

Finally, in closing this chapter, it is well worth noting that "change," as the cliché goes, "is a constant and ever-present reality." With that in mind, you need to be vigilant for changes in the business strategy that can affect your company's portfolio allocation groupings and investments. For example, if a new CEO comes in, puts a halt to a Transform-the-Business focus, and commits to a Grow-the-Business direction, the allocations to the portfolios and expectations of quality will change. Make sure that you frequently look at your Alignment Chart and ask yourself, "In light of any recent events or strategy changes, is this still a true picture?" If it is not, change the chart and communicate this change to your team.

Securing alignment as a new manager can be extremely valuable as a means of keeping yourself focused and your team anchored to the big picture. By exercising a little effort on a regular basis to keep track of key change indicators, you can maintain that alignment for both yourself and your team.

ACTION ITEMS:

Step 1: Go to the listed research sites and determine your company's key strategic objectives and how they plan to achieve them.

Step 2: Based on the company's objectives, group all of your IT investments into the appropriate portfolios.

Step 3: Based on which portfolio your team fits into, determine the strategy for the team (what they need to accomplish).

Step 4: Now, list what your team needs to do to achieve the objectives of the strategy.

Step 5: Next, list how you are going to make your team successful. What are you personally going to do?

Step 6: Review and finalize with your manager.

Step 7: Communicate, communicate, communicate!

3

GET TO KNOW YOUR PEOPLE

Nobody outside of a baby carriage or a judge's chamber believes in an unprejudiced point of view.

LILLIAN HELLMAN

Why is it important for you to know your people?

In the last century, American business invested in equipment. After all, we were in the Industrial Age, and our business equipment was our most valuable resource.

We upgraded and refurbished our equipment and machinery, built bigger and better manufacturing facilities, and added new equipment as it became available. We then hired skilled individuals to operate and maintain our new equipment and protect our sizable investment. We really focused on knowing how to support and get the most out of our equipment.

Today, we are living in the Information Age, and your company's most valuable assets are no longer its capital, land, or equipment, but rather its people and their creativity. It stands to reason, then, that getting to know your people, and making personal and monetary investments that keep them working at their highest, most creative, healthiest, most motivated levels of performance is the most prudent investment you can make.

Study after study has confirmed that effort and money invested in employees result in significantly increased performance, which, in turn, results in an overall increase in the growth of the company. The question, then, for you as a new IT manager is simply this: What can you do to help your employees perform at their peak? The answer is… a lot!

Your actions as the manager will have a powerful impact on your team

A couple of years ago, when the Gallup organization did an extensive study of what created employee satisfaction within organizations and resulted in workers' being engaged and staying, they found that you, the direct manager of the team, have the most influence in keeping people happy and anchored in an organization. In fact, they found that there were twelve basic truths that highly satisfied and engaged employees believed. Engaged employees believed the following to be true:

• I know what is expected of me at work.

- I have the materials and equipment I need to do my work right.
- At work, I have the opportunity to do what I do best every day.
- In the last seven days, I have received recognition or praise for doing good work.
- My supervisor, or someone at work, seems to care about me as a person.
- There is someone at work who encourages my development.
- At work, my opinions seem to count.
- The mission or purpose of my company makes me feel my job is important.
- My fellow employees are committed to doing quality work.
- I have a best friend at work.
- In the last six months, someone at work has talked to me about my progress.
- This last year, I have had opportunities at work to learn and grow.

The lesson here is simply that all of these engaging and job-satisfying conditions are created by you, the direct manager. In fact, we all know of people who left great companies because they did not like their manager, and other people who stayed in less than optimal companies because they had a great relationship with their manager. Simply put, the success of your company in the next millennium is largely dependent upon your ability to continually train, motivate, and retain your twenty-first century machinery—your people! (Hiring is another key component, but we have omitted it here since it is the topic of the next chapter.)

What exactly does it mean to know your people?

One of the biggest and most frequent blunders made by new IT managers is to mistake knowledge of surface trivia for "knowing their people," and to neglect truly getting to know their people. What we mean by "getting–to–know their people" is not just knowing their names and how many technical certifications they have in their Human Resources files. (Although this is important, to some degree, and some new managers ignore this as well.) What we are referring to is getting to know the members of the team as individual people.

It may seem repetitious, but this is such an important point that it bears constant reiteration: as a manager, your most valuable resource for getting results is your people. What is most important is your ability to take a group of people with diverse talents, drives, and strategies, and meld them into a productive force that is greater than the sum of its parts. Just as important as understanding how you and your team relate to the big picture, is the need for you to get to know your people.

By really getting to know your people, you will learn three important things:

- What your team is capable of doing.
- What makes them want to perform, or motivates them.
- The manner in which they think and will most likely perform.

Let's look at each one of these and see why they are so important to your success as a manager.

What they are capable of doing

According to an article that appeared in an issue of Fortune magazine, "Intellectual capital is becoming corporate America's most valuable asset and can be its sharpest competitive weapon." We've often heard that the most valuable assets of a company today walk in every morning and leave every night. The writer of that article, Thomas A. Stewart, goes on to say that "the challenge is to find what you have—and use it." The point is very simple. Wherever you have a team of people, you have a pool of intellectual capital. The issue for you as a manager is how to assess what you have, mine it, and turn it into productive value.

According to writers Donald O. Clifton and Paula Nelson in the 1992 book Soar with Your Strengths, too many managers spend their time trying to "round people out," instead of finding out what people are good at doing and having them do that all day long. The writers share a very simple yet powerful allegory about how a duck, a fish, an eagle, an owl, a squirrel, and a rabbit decide to create a human-like school system that will develop "well-rounded" animals that can effectively perform in the areas of running, swimming, tree-climbing, jumping, and flying. The results, of course, are funny, if not outright ludicrous. Nevertheless, this is what many new, and even a quite a few more experienced, managers seek to do when they try to create "well-rounded" employees.

We agree with the advice Clifton and Nelson give in the introduction to Part One of the book; "Let the rabbits run." In short, don't try to "round" your people, especially when you hardly know them. Get to know your people and their talents, and put the talents they have to good use.

What makes them want to perform, or motivates them

A second good reason to get to know your people is that it will enable you to be a more effective motivator. Motivating your team is another key function of management. If you do not motivate your people in their jobs, you will, at best, eke out a mediocre performance from them. In fact, according to the previously noted study by the Gallup organization, 71% of people who go to work every day are not fully engaged in their work. This means that only 29% of the workforce is fully engaged in their jobs. According to Curt Coffman, co-writer of First, Break All The Rules, "Engaged employees produce more, they make more money for the company, they create emotional engagement with the customers they serve, and they create environments where people are productive and accountable. We also know that engaged employees stay with the organization longer and are much more committed to quality and growth."

How does knowing your people enable you to motivate and fully engage them? Well, we are sure that you will agree that a working mother raising two kids will have a different set of drivers than a single woman trying to climb the corporate ladder. To the first woman, a trip 1,200 miles away from home for a two-week presentation to a key client could be a logistical nightmare. For the second, it might be the coveted assignment she has been waiting for, and an opportunity to display her talent and potential.

These dynamics are not static, either. For instance, let's say that you hire somebody who is clearly motivated by monetary rewards. For this person, a variable bonus might be really important. What is going on in his life at the time plays an important role in why he is focused on money; he has a fiancée and is saving for a wedding, as well as a house. But a year or two from now, that same employee, now your chief project manager, is no longer satisfied with a hefty bonus or variable pay. His life has changed, and now what he really wants is to be home more often so that he can spend more time with his newborn child.

The above may not be the case in every such instance, but the examples are given to make you aware of how the fluid personal dynamics in people's lives affect their jobs. The point is to make you aware that these dynamics exist, evolve, and that, in addition to getting to know a person, you need to have an ongoing relationship with him/her in order to keep a finger on the pulse of your team.

As people evolve and go through different life situations, their values, as well as the things they focus on, will change. You have to be aware of this, because the reward systems and the things that you are doing in order to keep your people engaged must change as well, in order to resonate with their new needs. You need to stay tuned to each person and his/her needs. To do this, you need to keep your eyes and ears open for how your people are evolving and growing.

Top managers make a practice of connecting with each of their people on a daily basis, whenever possible. This way they know immediately if something is wrong. If you know a person well and you ask them how they are doing, even if they force a smile and say "fine," you'll know if something is not right. You can then probe further to find out why they are out of sorts, and help them so that they can become less preoccupied by the problem and more engaged in the tasks at hand.

Know the manner in which they think and will most likely perform!

Finally, a third good reason for getting to know your people is that you will become familiar with their preferred style of thinking and behaving within specific situations. Who loves to do research? Who is action-oriented? Who is a great "devil's advocate" who can find the other side of what seems like an open and shut case? Who is great at negotiating concessions and diplomatically finding an accepted middle ground? Knowing a person's preferred way of thinking and behaving will give you another dimension to consider when doing one of the most important things you will do as an effective manager—selecting the right person to do a job.

We think that by now the reasons for supporting and getting to know your people are probably very clear. The question then is, "How do you do it?"

Starting and maintaining activities that let you support and get to know your people

Jim – Working with companies as a coach, I've come across a number of simple ways good managers support and get to know their people. For example:

A "book-of-the-month" program. This could be as simple as buying a few books on a key topic that is relevant to the team, reading them, and then discussing potential applications.

Starting an audiocassette library or joining a low-cost tape rental club.

Arranging for speakers to come in and give seminars.

Providing external coaches for your key people.

These are not high price tag items. I have, however, seen them produce huge returns.

Three things you can do

There are many things that you can do to support your team, and at the same time, gain and maintain insights about the knowledge, motivations, patterns of thinking, and behavior of the individuals that make up your team. Here are three things you can do to begin:

- Conduct employee-focused one-on-one meetings/discussions.
- Facilitate regular networking events.
- Take part in a group personality assessment.

Let's take a closer look at these.

1. Hold employee-focused one-on-one meetings

No matter how busy you are, please make time to meet with each of your people on a one-to-one basis as often as you can. By this, we mean a scheduled thirty to forty-five-minute meeting to gauge personal drivers and to discuss what each individual needs to succeed and meet goals. These discussions are separate from work-related "updates," progress meetings, or annual reviews. While these are also needed, they do not take the place of the employee-focused one-on-one.

Questions you can ask during an employee-focused one-on-one include:

How are you and your family?

Is there anything you feel you need from me to help you with your current project/work?

Do you see any job or development opportunities that you would like to explore?

Do you see the next step for you in this company? (If the answer is no, help him/her brainstorm.)

Please note that the personal question at the beginning of this list is not there by accident. The more you know your people and genuinely care about them—both at work and in their personal lives—the more effective a manager you will become. If an individual is having a serious problem at home, it's going to affect his/her work. An employee who just found out that his/her parent has a serious illness cannot and will not be focused on the team's work until he/she is able to find a means of coping with the personal challenge. Despite the myth that people should leave their personal lives at home, this is easier said than done. We are, after all, holistic units. Where one part goes, there the rest will follow.

Business guru Tom Peters talks about the fact that twenty or so years ago, companies adopted a posture that work was work, and that employees should leave personal problems at the door when they arrived at work. Clearly this was nonsense. It does not work, and companies and managers that stuck with that philosophy paid dearly for it. As a result their people developed the attitude, "If you don't care about me, then I don't care about you!" They then resolved to do the minimum required to keep their jobs, but little else above and beyond. Later, when the same companies wanted their people to take an active interest in the organization, the people were completely disengaged and deaf to their call. On the other hand, the more successful companies have been those with managers who recognize the value in their people, and nurture the "holistic" individual. The point is simply this: by taking a "complete" interest in your people's needs and working with them to address those needs, you will do much toward increasing the overall productive capacity of your team.

After asking one of these questions, we recommend that you listen to both the answer and how the answer is delivered. Your mantra during this listening exercise should be, as famous self-help author and speaker Wayne Dyer once said, "How may I serve? How may I serve?" Your team member should be doing most of the talking in this meeting, while you listen. Your goal is to determine how to best coach, support, and promote the interests of the person, while aligning them with the needs and interests of your company (creating the old cliché win/win situation).

Have you ever replied in a joking manner to a question like,

"How are you doing today?" with a remark like, "Terrible, I just lost my left kidney!" to which the questioner replied, "Great! Have a nice day!" While this may seem funny, it also forms the basis for many of the disconnected discussions between managers and their team members, in which real listening doesn't take place. Good managers really listen to their team members. Superior managers totally "tune-in" and assess when and how they are needed.

"Tuning-in" is a deep form of listening used by coaches and other people in professions in which really taking in what someone else is communicating is vital to being effective. Tuning-in results in literally turning all of your attention to the other speaker. It means suspending your personal judgment and listening with your feelings as well as with your ears. It means hearing that which is not said or is non-verbally communicated. It involves listening for emotional tone as well as spoken content. Learning to become fully tuned-in can be one of the best tools you as a manager can use to fully connect with your people. We recommend that you invest a little bit of time learning some "tuning-in" techniques. (To learn more about "tuning-in," refer to one of the several coaching books listed in the resource section at the end of this book.)

You will find that of all the things you can do to get to know your people, this one-on-one approach, combined with "tuning-in," is probably one of the singularly most important components.

Joe – One of the things I started doing several years ago, after reading a study about the degree of disconnectedness between managers and their team members, was to hold one-on-ones with everyone on my team. When I first came on board as a manager of a team, I would send out a note requesting thirty to forty-five minutes of their time to get acquainted. In the note inviting each team member to meet with me, I would point out that this was an informal "agenda-less" meeting, meant to give us an opportunity to get to know each other. I would introduce myself and share a few things about my background—both business and personal—as well as what I thought were my talents, where I felt I needed help, and my patterns of thinking and behaving. During the meeting, I would learn about their school background, marital and parental status, as well as other personal and professional tidbits. It was this information that enabled me to place people in positions, with reward systems that motivated my people to top performance. One of these teams went from being a low-productivity group under the microscope of management to a highly-charged and award-winning team. Another disgruntled group metamorphosed into the most admired team in the company. They were basically all the same people. All I did was take the square pegs out of the round holes and put them into square holes that suited them better.

2. Host regular networking events

Another excellent tool that will help you gain insight into your people, while building relationships, is to stage regular networking events for your team. Networking events are valuable because they enable you to see your team members as they interact with the rest of the group. This will offer you other perspectives into their knowledge, motivations, and patterns of thinking and behaving.

To stage a successful networking event, first find out what topics are of common interest to your team members. Next, stage a non-mandatory get-together—non-mandatory being key. If people feel that they must come to this event because it is required by the boss, they will not come with an open mind. Even if it means having low attendance in the beginning, make attendance voluntary. If the event is good, word will get out and attendance will rise.

By the way, make sure that the focus of the meeting is always on topics that bring value to your team members. Bring in speakers to discuss subjects that may be of interest to them, including pension plan options, company-sponsored training tools, medical plan choices, and certification opportunities. Do not let this become a meeting where you discuss new policies or procedures. If you have some quick announcements, make them, but do not shift the focus of this meeting from giving them value and helping them build a relationship with you and each other to a boring recitation of rules and regulations. (There is a time and place for these. It is important to do this, but not in this meeting.)

Make sure you secure a meeting place where people can arrive fifteen to twenty minutes before the scheduled presentation and linger for about fifteen to twenty minutes after the scheduled presentation. You want to promote unstructured networking among team members, and between you and your team members.

As simple as the concept is, it works. Listening to a speaker on a topic of personal value and interest, then allowing time for networking, is a very powerful team insight and cohesiveness building tool.

> **Joe** – As part of an effort to bring together a scattered team of people, I started a program dubbed "The Lunch and Learn." The Lunch and Learn program was very simple. Every other week, we would gather as a team for lunch and listen to a presentation on a topic that I felt was of interest and value to my team members. This was not a status meeting, or a meeting in which we discussed specific work the team members did and/or the quality of that work. The focus of the meeting was on the team's needs.
>
> For example, we had people who managed the company's 401K speak about maximizing their savings investments. Another speaker informed us about opportunities to use company resources to learn and develop new skills that could lead to possible promotions. We also brought in outside speakers to discuss a variety of subjects. The results were fantastic. Not only did the team members working on different projects begin to bond and form supportive relationships, but I also developed strong personal relationships with each team member, which fostered a strong sense of teamwork and cooperation.

3. Take a group personality assessment

If your company will sponsor it, we highly recommend that you and your team sign up for any of the many group personality assessment programs. Whether you prefer Myers-Briggs, Keirsey, or the Enneagram, what is most important and of value is conducting a team personality assessment. By the way, you should definitely participate.

Not only will you find this a fun discovery process, it will also take you a long way toward getting to know your people and developing strategies for benefiting from, instead of stumbling upon their unique differences. The resulting understanding and bonding is well worth it.

> **Joe** – I worked for a management team some years ago in which our manager decided to do a group assessment. At first, I was a bit reluctant, not only because I was busy and could not see the immediate value of doing this, but also because the idea of having myself and others assessed as a group did not feel totally comfortable. As it turned out, not only was it fun, but it also enabled the team to work better with our manager and each other. In fact, it reduced a great deal of the tension produced by our differences in perception and style. Many times, when one of us was in full court displaying our dominant traits, the others would jokingly point it out and then look for ways to utilize this trait as a strength ingredient.

Closing thoughts on the value of getting to know your people

It bears repeating that in today's world, where clearly a lot of what organizations consider capital resides in the heads of the employees, as a manager, you've got a pretty big job. The more you can tap into the capabilities of your people and focus them on the needs of the company, the more effective you will be as a capital builder. Truly, one of the best ways that you can drive value into your company is by developing your human capital resources. There is no better way to do this than by you, the direct manager, making it a high priority to fully get to know and support your people.

ACTION ITEMS:

1. Schedule thirty to forty-five-minute one-on-one sessions with each of your new team members.

2. Develop an employee-focused networking event. Come up with three topics and potential speakers. Test these by talking to some of your team members to make sure the topics and speakers will be of interest to the team.

3. Find out if your Human Resources department uses a consultant or a consulting group that does personality assessments. Volunteer yourself and your team for an assessment.

4. Explore setting up a "Lunch and Learn" program in your office. If your group is too small, you might partner with some other teams within the organization and share the cost. These talks do not always have to be company-related. The purpose is to develop the individual team members and strengthen the synergy of the team.

If you need help with any of these programs,
please contact The Bentley Partnership at
employeelearning@bentleypartnership.com.

4

HIRE THE BEST PEOPLE

I don't hire people who have to be told to be nice. I hire nice people.

LEONA HELMSLEY

No matter how wonderful you are as a manager, or how great the salary and benefits your company offers, positions will open up and you will have to hire people. Because one of the keys to success as a manager is having good people working on your team, hiring the right people is a very important skill to hone. In this chapter, you will learn how to build and sustain your most important asset, an A-Team.

Our language today has become full of phrases like companies saying they want to be "employers of choice," and magazines telling potential employees that they will teach them how to be "employees of choice." The fact of the matter is that choices about who you want to hire, and for whom people prefer to work, are an individual matter predicated primarily on the following key variables:

1. Skills and competence

2. Motivations

Joe Sabrin, founder and Executive Vice President of eHire, a Manhattan-based recruiting firm, advises new managers to start their new role by developing a staffing plan.

A staffing plan is an excellent start to gaining specificity in terms of the skills and competence levels needed by the team. After looking at the staffing plan model, we will explore ways to identify and test for the presence of the motivations we need in our new hires in order to develop and maintain our A-Team, followed by options for finding people.

How to build a skill database or "staffing plan"

A staffing plan is the result of looking at some very basic information about what you need to meet the required functions of your team, who you have on your team, and the gaps in between. A staffing plan will tell you whom you need to find in order to fill gaps, and whom you need in your future "pipeline" in case you need a replacement due to a promotion or departure. The table below will give you a basic overview of the layout of a staffing plan

Functions/Key Areas	People & Skills In Place	Gaps	Pipeline
Take this directly from the functional requirements section of your Alignment chart. For the sake of this example, let's use generic labels and say that your team requires the skills a, b, c, d, e, and f. Each skill should be possessed by at least two members to ensure backup.	*Under the names of each staff member, list the requirements that each staff member addresses.* **Team Member 1** • skill a • skill c • skill b • skill d **Team Member 2** • skill a • skill c • skill e **Team Member 3** • Skill a • skill d • skill e **Team Member 4** • skill a • skill e	A quick look at these two columns tells you that you need to acquire skill *F* in two people because none of the current team members has it. That means either quickly training two people, or hiring a person with the skill and then training a backup. You also need to train or hire a backup for skill *B*, since only one person has that skill.	This manager needs to maintain a pipeline for skills a, b, c, d, e, and f. She may also notice that some of the team members are disengaged or ready for a change. If she sees this, then she must move the skills that person possess to the front of the pipeline.

As you can see, a simple staffing plan enables you to see how ready you are to address the demands of the function with your current supply, and to plan accordingly. If you've already prepared an "Alignment Chart," and have made a start in getting to know your people (specifically, their skills, capabilities, and competencies), you have the information needed to input into a staffing plan model. Even though you may feel you intuitively know what you need, please don't skip this step. By putting your information into a staffing plan model, you will find it will yield a great number of insights into your current and future needs.

Three common issues you can avoid by having a staffing plan

In addition to making you aware of current and future skill needs, a staffing plan will help you to consciously avoid some of the most common mistakes new IT managers make, which can erode the quality and productivity of their teams. Let's take a look at the most common three.

Mistake #1

The first and biggest mistake, of course, is hiring unqualified people for the wrong reasons.

> **Jim** — One of the saddest realities I've learned about corporate America is that people who are considered "good-looking" are hired more often and faster than their perhaps "less attractive" counterparts. Unless you're casting for a commercial or hiring models, this should not be your main criterion. Not only is it discriminating and terribly unfair, but it's downright foolish. You may well be passing up great people just to have a good-looking staff. Having a clear picture of what you are seeking will keep you focused on what is relevant. Sabrin points out that new managers frequently hire unqualified people because they do not really know what they need, and therefore, they end up hiring people based on personal affinities that have nothing to do with what the job requires.

According to Sabrin, one of the most common manifestations of this is hiring people because they went to your old school, or because they like the same non-work activities. "Instead of hiring to fill a job, they basically hire a buddy," says Sabrin.

Mistake #2

The second mistake made by hiring managers without a staffing plan, according to Sabrin, is changing the duties of the job, after hiring a candidate, when they discover other things that need to be done that they did not foresee before bringing the person on board. "Nothing will start a relationship off on the wrong foot like changing a new hire's duties after (s)he has been hired. This will most likely be perceived as, worst case, "bait-and-switch," and best case, incompetence on the part of the hiring manager," according to Sabrin. Again, the most common cause is that the hiring manager is a new manager going through the "needs" discovery process, while engaged in hiring without a staffing plan.

Mistake #3

The third mistake is starting a hiring process, and then aborting it because you don't have a real job ready. Managers who do this will get a reputation, according to Sabrin, for being either unreliable or lacking in integrity. In either case, the better candidates will get word and avoid them. Most of the time this happens because the manager discovers that the person (s)he needed is already on the team. So again, a staffing plan can prevent this, as well as avoiding the cost of wasted time.

Point: A hiring plan is an essential dimension of the manager's hiring toolkit

All of these hiring errors offer a fast track for losing the respect and support of your team, as well as of potential candidates. A hiring plan can easily help you to avoid these mistakes, and can take you a long way toward hiring the right people, for the right job, at the right time. While a hiring plan is very important, it is really only one dimension of the manager's hiring toolkit. Let's focus our discussion now on another dimension that we feel is as important as knowing the skills needed to create a successful A-Team. This too often ignored dimension, to the detriment of hiring managers, is the motivation or desire of the job candidate to do the particular job.

In addition to skills, don't overlook the role of motivation in success

Joe – For more than fifteen years, I've made it a practice to hire motivation over skill and I've never been disappointed. I once hired a young lady as my Operations Assistant who did not even know how to use a spreadsheet program that was part of the job, over other candidates who were accomplished pros with the software. The reason I hired her was for her personal desire to do the work. Her clear honesty and positive can-do outlook told me that once she learned the basics she would run rings around the others, just flying on the fuel of pure enthusiasm. My hunch proved right, and she has turned out to be one of my strongest team supporters. Another common mistake made by managers when they hire people is that if they do focus on skills, they do so exclusively and ignore other important factors. Basically, they look only at what the person can do, and ignore a lot of questions like "Will they want to do this?" or "Do they have the motivation to do this?"

Just because someone can do something, doesn't mean that they want to do it. On the other hand, a candidate who lacks a high degree of expertise in a specific skill may still have the motivation and passion to leave the more experienced candidate in the dust, in terms of performance, after a short ramp-up period. In addition to looking for specific work experience, we recommend that you determine whether your candidate is motivated to do the things you need done. Let's explore this more closely.

What can you do to determine the motivations you need in your ideal candidate?

We recommend that before you start the hiring process, you prepare a job description that, in addition to listing the skills needed based on your hiring plan, includes a profile of the type of motivation you need in the ideal candidate. For example, if you need someone to help you with an innovative project that requires exploring a lot of new ground and taking some measure of career risk, you obviously want someone who is adventurous and loves challenges. On the other hand, if the position calls for meticulous care in following specific procedures without deviation, this same person could be the wrong candidate. (In the second case, you would want someone who is more careful and security-oriented.)

This is where you can employ the same techniques you learned in Chapter One to build a general picture of the IT manager job. Below is an example of a generic driver profile for a Help Desk agent role (assuming, of course, that you are the IT Help Desk manager looking for a Help Desk agent):

Generic Help Desk Agent Driver—Primary Talents/Gifts/Mindset Profile

What does a Help Desk agent need to be able to do easily?

- Determine the next step in problem resolution, based on a telephone conversation.
- Properly handle a variety of people, who are usually upset over a problem when they call.
- Handle multiple tasks

What do good Help Desk agents generally love to do, that makes them feel rewarded by this role?

- Solve problems.
- Take ownership of issues and challenges.
- Help people.

- What tend to be some of the goals of people who are successful in this role?
- To be heroes.
- To talk with a number of different people.
- To handle multiple transactions per day.

What do good Help Desk agents generally do naturally, almost automatically?

- Key in on the emotional state of another person and gain diplomatic, but firm, control over the flow of the conversation.
- Arrive at a workable solution, or determine who to send to fix a problem, based on collected information.
- Remain positive and enthusiastic, despite dealing with unhappy and irritated people on a regular basis throughout the course of each day.

Let's fine tune and complete the picture of the person you are looking for, by listing the skills you seek (taken out of your hiring plan), followed by a list of the motivations this person needs to have.

Help Desk Agent Search Profile

Skill

- Knows how to enter information and use XYZ Help Desk activity tracking system.
- Five years' experience supporting our basic operating systems.
- Three years' experience supporting our word processor, spreadsheet, and project applications.

Qualities

- Highly empathetic problem-solver.
- Enjoys working with people and helping them solve problems.

• Enjoys a day full of a variety of different problem-solving activities.

You now have a more complete picture of what you need. Armed with this picture, you are less likely to hire someone who has all of the skills, but likes to work on one project for an entire month without distraction, or someone who hates having others dump issues on him/her (which, after all, is what happens at a Help Desk all day long). This is not to say that someone who likes to stay focused on one thing without distraction is never a good employee, but simply that they would clearly not be the right person for this specific job. The next thing you need to do is find the candidate who matches your needs.

How can you determine if your candidate has "the right motivational stuff?"

To test for the presence of the right motivational stuff in your candidates, you can ask probing questions, such as, "What's most important to you in a job?" You can steadily probe with this type of question until you hear two or three key themes emerging. This will give you some insight into what makes each candidate feel fulfilled. Using the previous profile as our target, if you notice a great deal of focus on helping people solve problems, nurturing, and being empathetically supportive of others, you may have a potential "motivational fit."

In addition to this, you can also use "behavioral interview" questions. Unlike the traditional interview questions such as "Tell me about yourself," behavioral interviewers ask questions such as "Give me an example of a time when you had to use your fact-finding skills to solve a problem while under a lot of pressure from a customer?" Or you can ask "Describe to me your most recent work accomplishment?" By listening to the response, as well as how the candidate responds, you will get a better picture of how they work and how their motivation fits or does not fit your needs. (Most people will relate accomplishments that they enjoyed and which brought them deep personal satisfaction. By knowing what produces these feelings in your candidate, you will gain a great deal of insight into the person and how they may or may not fit into the role you need to fill.)

To get you started, here are a few examples of behavioral interview questions:

Describe for me your most recent accomplishment.

Give me a specific example of a time when you used your good judgment and logic in solving a problem.

Describe a situation in which you used your persuasive skills to successfully convince someone to see things your way.

Describe a situation in which you anticipated potential problems and proactively developed preventative measures.

Tell me about a time when you had to use your communication skills to influence someone's opinion or decision.

Give me an example of a time when you had to make a split-second decision.

Give me a specific example of how you motivated others.

Give me a specific example of a time when you had to conform to a policy with which you did not agree.

Tell me about a time when you had too many things to do and how you prioritized your tasks.

Give me a specific example of a time when you showed initiative and took the lead.

Please discuss the most important written document that you have ever been required to complete.

Give me an example of how you handled missing an obvious solution to a problem in the past.

Give me a specific example of a time when you set a goal and were able to proudly meet or achieve it.

Tell me about a specific situation in which you had to deal with a very upset customer or co-worker.

Tell me about a time when you had to go above and beyond the call of duty in order to get your job done.

Give me a specific example of a situation in which something you tried to accomplish failed, and how you handled the failure.

Give me a specific example of a time when you used your fact-finding skills to solve a problem.

Give me a specific example of how you dealt with a person whom you knew did not like you.

Give me an example of how you've dealt with conflict.

Tell me about the most difficult decision you have made in the last year.

You can pick two or three of these, or use these to fashion your own script that probes for the motivational qualities you seek for a particular role. So, continuing with our Help Desk agent example, you may want to use the following four questions:

Tell me about a specific situation in which you had to deal with a very upset customer or co-worker.

Give me a specific example of a time when you used your fact-finding skills to solve a problem.

Give me a specific example of how you dealt with a person whom you knew did not like you.

Describe for me your most recent accomplishment.

Now that you've learned how to prepare and use a staffing plan to identify the specific skills you need, identify the right motivational drivers, and test for the presence of the right motivational drivers in order to develop your A-Team, the next question is pretty practical and basic: "Where do you go to find people when you need them?"

Where to look for people when you need to hire staff

There are many ways to prospect for new team members. Your

company may have policies in place that dictate how and where you should go. Make sure you understand and adhere to these.

In some cases, the company will let you choose from among a menu of choices. The most common places where your company will let you look for people to fill positions include:

- The corporate website's help wanted section.

- Employee referral programs. These are programs that pay employees a fee for referring other people to the company.

- Job sites on the Internet, such as Monster Board, Hot Site, and Career Builders.

- Publication help wanted advertising. Placing ads in The Wall Street Journal or The New York Times are examples of this.

- Staffing companies. Using companies that provide short and long-term temporary or contracting arrangements.

- Traditional recruiters (also called "headhunters").

According to industry experts like Sabrin, the cost of recruiting can vary widely based on the model. "Without external help, the cost can range from eight to ten thousand dollars, compared to eighteen to twenty-four thousand dollars with external help," adds Sabrin. So why even consider the higher cost models? The answer is the differences in quality. Each model offers its own pluses and minuses. The right one for you will be predicated on your company's needs. The chart below summarizes the basic distinctions between these models.

Method	Pluses and Minuses
Corporate Website	**Pluses** - Low cost **Minuses** - Low visibility, unless you invest in promoting - Low morale if you don't offer the job internally first - May take a long time to find the right person
Referrals	**Pluses** - Low cost **Minuses** - People recommend and market their friends (see Joe's comment below) - May take a long time to find the right person
Job Sites	**Pluses** - Low cost **Minuses** - Lack of filtering and focus - You will be avalanched by resumes - May take a long time to find the right person
Advertising (e.g. *The Wall Street Journal* and *The New York Times*)	**Pluses** - Low cost **Minuses** - Lack of filtering and focus - You will be avalanched by resumes - May take a long time to find the right person

In the end, these are the lowest cost solutions, but they offer low quality (They also offer low-quality candidates, since most employed people who are at the top of their fields do not seek jobs via these avenues.) Let's now look at the pricier models, in which you as the hiring manager employ some outside help.

Method	Pluses and Minuses
Staffing Companies	**Pluses** Faster access to a person with the skills to do the job Less of your time spent hunting for a candidate **Minuses** You will pay a premium for having the person on staff for the entire period of time that you have them You will be subject to the impact on the individual of their company's employment policies (So if they work for a "stingy" company and they become disgruntled due to a bad raise, you will inherit the attitude problem.)
Traditional Recruiters	**Pluses** Faster access to person with the skills to do the job Less of your time spent hunting for a candidate Access to a large pool of candidates, including those currently employed **Minuses** This is obviously one of the most expensive routes If the candidate leaves after less than ninety days, you lose the entire fee and will probably have to come up with a second fee to replace them

The key benefits of these models are speed, the fact that they require less of your personal focus, and the fact that you get access to a pool of candidates that includes people who are currently working and may not be looking for a job. The downside, of course, is higher up-front costs.

> **Joe** – Joe Sabrin's company eHire (www.ehire.com) actually offers a sixth choice. They combine the personal touch of traditional recruiting with the speed and efficiency of Internet technology. They believe that personal service will always be a necessary part of the recruiting process, so their model is set up to provide personal attention to each client's needs. They also form relationships with candidates to whom they provide advice and guidance. eHire screens each candidate, usually in person, to assure that they meet or exceed the clients' requirements. Clients only receive resumes from candidates who are truly qualified for their positions. On the other end, candidates are given an honest appraisal of their skills, background, and what they are worth in the marketplace. Each job opportunity is presented to the candidate before a resume is sent to the client. In effect, eHire uses the Internet as a low-cost processing engine, while employing a traditional agency touch in terms of guiding hiring managers and candidates through the search process. As a result, they offer a low-cost alternative with predictable service costs and longer-than-average fee return guarantees (the average is 90 days; eHire offers 120). Here is how they stack up:

Pluses:

- Faster access to a person with the skills to do the job.
- Less of your time spent hunting for a candidate.
- Access to a larger pool of candidates, including those currently employed.
- Use of the Internet as a processing agent reduces costs.
- Longer trial period mitigates risks.

- Fixed-contract pricing makes costs predictable.
- Intimate support through the use of Account Relationship Managers.

Minuses:

- It's a new model, so you would be pioneering a bit.

Closing thoughts on hiring

It bears repeating that hiring will be a regular part of your life as a manager. Becoming skillful in all aspects of the process will enhance the potential for success of you and your team. These important aspects of hiring include, but are not limited to:

- Always having an updated staffing plan.
- Knowing the skills and motivational drivers you need, and knowing how to identify the people who possess what you need.
- Using the most effective means of finding candidates.

If you follow these simple steps, you will be well on your way toward building, developing, and sustaining your A-Team.

ACTION ITEMS:

1. Prepare a "staffing plan" for your team.

2. If you need to fill positions, develop a profile of the ideal candidate(s), including motivational drivers.

3. Identify a minimum of two sources you will use to look for candidates.

5

GIVING FEEDBACK

Avoiding danger is no safer in the long run than exposure.

HELEN KELLER

Why is giving feedback an important process that is often avoided?

Joe – A few years ago, I sat in on a team meeting in which one of the team members proceeded to bully the other members, cutting them off when they tried to speak and just being plain rude. The manager of the team sat there looking very uncomfortable, but not taking any action to curb the behavior or restore some semblance of order. During a break in the meeting, I approached the manager and pointed out that this team member's behavior was distracting and inappropriate. He told me that he had been "living with this problem for a few months now, and it was getting worse." What I found in talking to this manager was that he did not have a strategy for dealing with this issue. I coached him through scripting a corrective feedback session, and I am glad to say that in two subsequent meetings I attended with this manager and this team member present, the team member was actually very well-behaved. The manager could have saved himself a great deal of embarrassment and pain had he known how to address this earlier.

People by nature avoid anything that could lead to an uncomfortable confrontation. As a result, most new managers avoid giving their team members feedback. Many managers have trouble communicating corrective feedback to their staff, and find it difficult to even provide general performance feedback during reviews and other occasions.

In this chapter, we are going to discuss how you can effectively give feedback. Feedback is an important part of what you as a manager must provide to your team. Remember that being a manager means playing the role of the coach of the team. A silent coach who does not provide the team with his/her perspective is not a valuable coach.

Like most of the skills used by managers, giving feedback is learnable. In fact, the more feedback-giving strategies you learn, the more versatile you will become in your ability to provide the right feedback in any situation. Let's focus on addressing the toughest type of feedback you will need to give from time to time, corrective feedback.

The five things to remember when giving corrective feedback

Most new managers fear that if they give corrective feedback, they will sound like they are scolding another adult. Perhaps they had the unfortunate experience of witnessing such an event, or being subjected to it by a manager in the past. As a result of this negative picture, they avoid what they view as a potentially very uncomfortable situation, and at times, permit unchecked problems to escalate. Below are five steps for providing corrective feedback:

1. **Do not react with anger.** Make sure your own temper and behavior are in check. Do not scold. Remember, "barking rights" are old hat, and besides, they won't produce results unless you simply want the person to leave.

2. **Start on a positive note.** Explain to the person why (s)he is of value to you. Make sure you communicate that the reason you are taking corrective action is that you value the person, and expect more from him/her.

3. **Focus your attention on correcting the problem**, and not on remodeling the person. Be very specific about the behavior you want changed. Describe what is not acceptable. Stick with correcting this specific behavior. Do not imply or state, in any way, that the behavior to be corrected is the result of any personal character flaw in your team member.

4. **Tell the person exactly what you expect.** Describe what you want.

5. **Give the person responsibility** for fixing the problem and a specific timetable for making visible improvements.

Corrective feedback example

The following is an example of a fictitious manager, Don, giving his equally fictitious team member, Jack, corrective feedback about cutting off other team members in a meeting.

Don – Jack, I need to talk to you about something. It won't take more than five minutes.

Jack – Oh, what is it?

Don – Jack, as you know, I value you highly as an expert in application design. I think you are one of the best on my team. During this last team meeting, you interrupted the other members every time they tried to speak. Naturally, I find this disruptive to my meeting, as well as to my efforts to hear everybody out. It is unacceptable. I want you to follow the same protocol as everyone else as we go around the table. If you have something to add after your turn, please wait until the person speaking has finished, and then offer your comment or question.

Jack – I didn't know I was being disruptive. It's just that I have more experience than the others, and I felt that some of them were getting stuck on points.

Don – I appreciate your wealth of experience, as I am sure the team does, but I want to get their views and perspectives as well. I would like you to take the experience you have and add to it the simple process of following the meeting's rules of order. I think that will greatly increase the value that you bring to me, as well as to the team.

Jack – Sure Don. I want to help.

Don — I know you do, and that's why I felt it was worthwhile for us to have this discussion. Let's just put this into play in next week's meeting, okay?

Jack — Yes, of course.

Don – Thanks, Jack.

While all corrective feedback sessions may not go as smoothly as this one between Don and Jack, you will be surprised at how little resistance you get when you are diplomatic, yet direct. Most people want to be good team members and respond well to feedback. Most of the time, when a person does something that is really disruptive, there are underlying reasons which will come out during your corrective feedback discussion. This is an opportunity for you to get to know this person better, and in the process, improve your working relationship.

So now that we've tackled the most difficult type of feedback, let's take a look at a more routine type of feedback that you will need to give, performance feedback, and how you can get the most out of performance feedback sessions.

How to give effective general performance feedback

From time to time, and at least once a year, you will be given an opportunity to sit down with your employees, provide them with summative feedback on the past year's performance, and plan for the coming year. What you have to say about the previous year's performance should not be a surprise to your team members. If it is, you have not been communicating well with them throughout the year.

Your goal should be to use this as a development session, in which you and your staff member share your perspectives on the previous year's performance, and mutually plan for his/her activities and goals for the coming year.

Here are a few important things to keep in mind when providing performance feedback:

Do not
- Do all the talking.
- Use hearsay, especially if the comment relates to an area that requires attention or correction.
- Rate your team member on goals you did not communicate.

Do
- Talk about their strengths.

• Ask for their input on how you rated them.

• Talk about how they can build on their strengths.

One way you can set the stage for a better, more productive, and more interesting performance feedback meeting is by using some of the questions listed below, taken from Kurt Wright's book *Breaking the Rules.*

What special strengths do you feel might have played a key role in helping you achieve some of the results you attained this year?

Among your many job accomplishments during the past six months, which one or two do you feel most strongly about or consider most meaningful?

What key personal strengths or success factors can you identify that may have played an important role in helping you accomplish the above?

What are some special ways you can think of to put these personal strengths and success factors to work in other areas of your job?

What might be the benefits of your doing so for the team and the company?

How would you describe what your performance might look like, if all aspects were done ideally?

What steps would you need to take to bring your actual performance on a daily basis into alignment with the ideal you've just described?

What aspects of your job would you most like to be doing better?

The benefits of using these questions as part of a performance feedback session are many.

This type of questioning:

Fully engages the team member in the review process.

Fully engages the team member in developing goals that fit

his/her strengths and motivations, while driving value to the company.

Helps to expand the team member's appreciation of his/her strengths, and how to apply them to get results.

Enables you and the team member to build more of a shared perspective on goals and attainments. (Often referred to as "getting on the same page.")

Engenders an open discussion, where no one's agenda limits the discussion (and the possibility for coming up with creative ways to add value is not limited).

The subject of feedback is, of course, much larger than this small chapter containing the essential foundations. We highly recommend that you read books such as *Leadership and the One Minute Manager* by Patricia Zigarmi, Drea Zigarmi, and Kenneth H. Blanchard. Also, talk to your company's HR team and find out if they have a relationship with the Ken Blanchard Companies, or would be willing to send you to one of Blanchard's Situational Leadership training courses. You will find that the course is a worthwhile investment that will pay huge dividends in the development of your skills in partnering with and supporting your people. You can reach the Ken Blanchard Companies at 800-728-6000 (international callers can use 760-839-8070). Or you can visit them on the web at www.kenblanchard.com.

As a manager, knowing how to give various types of feedback will be a vital component of your success. We urge you to make a continuous lifetime study of this important topic.

ACTION ITEMS:

1. Using the corrective feedback example, write a few scripts of your own that you can use as templates for structuring corrective discussion around some of the most common challenges that come up in managing your team.

2. Pick out a few of the performance review questions to use the next time you sit down privately with a team member to discuss his/her performance and plans.

3. Try structuring a few questions of your own, along the same line of thinking as Kurt Wright's questions, which you think will be useful for you with your team.

4. Find out if your company offers or sponsors programs that will enable you to become a better performance partner with your team members.

6

LEARNING THE FINE ART OF BUYING I.T.

Experience teaches slowly and at the cost of mistakes.
JAMES A. FROUDE

Why you need to develop skills as a buyer of IT products and services

As an IT manager, you will be asked from time to time to either participate in or lead the effort to buy technology products or services. While this chapter will not make you an expert corporate buyer of IT services, it will provide you with the information you need to avoid the most common, and sometimes career-devastating, blunders.

> **Joe** – Here are two stories that drive home the need for managers to become savvy buyers of IT products and services. The first involves a gentleman I met a number of years ago who was a new technology manager. He told me a story about an experience he had when his new role required him to buy technology hardware for his company.
>
> At the time, his company was in the process of moving off a service they had been using, and needed to have a local area network put into place that would enable them to run their own applications. This LAN would also need to take over some of the functions that the service company had been handling.
>
> This new manager went out and called all the different companies who had the technology he needed to create the solution. After conducting his research, he chose the technologies that had the best features, called some of the companies, asked a few questions, and then made a selection—all of this in record time.
>
> Coming from a technical background, the manager knew to test the equipment before putting it out to be used by "live" end-users. Upon setting up all the equipment, this new manager was horrified to learn that even though everything "worked," there was no communication between the different boxes—essential in a local area network. He later found out that different companies were involved in creating the applications and hardware, and that the one thing that hadn't been

developed yet was the communication protocol which would enable these different pieces of equipment to speak to each other.

Fortunately for him, he had a couple of friends who belonged to an online bulletin board where people who developed freeware could exchange ideas. One of the items that had been developed was a small tool for enabling communications between the particular boxes he had purchased. As he had nothing to lose, he experimented with the product and actually got the whole system working.

The second incident involved a friend of mine who was looking for a supplier company to fix their various computers. After going through the selection process, they picked a company because it was advertised as "Macintosh certified." Since they had a couple of Macintosh computers in a department that was important to the company, they decided to go with this supplier.

When the first Macintosh call came in, they called their new service company to come in and fix the problem. They ended up waiting three days before they actually got serviced. This was not exactly what they had expected. A team member later found out from a friend at a professional association that the reason the company was Macintosh certified was because one of their hundreds of technicians had a Macintosh certification.

So one of the things that we need to do when buying technology services is to be very savvy about what they are offering, and really understand what they have in terms of not only their capability, but their capacity as well. Through this process, both of these people learned that the most reliable source for securing that information was their peers who had used the technology or service.

How to put your IT "buyer" education on the fast track

One of the easiest ways to learn a new skill or process is often the last to come to mind. The answer is really simple. If you want to become really good at doing something, like buying IT products and services, find someone who is already an expert at it and ask them how they do it. Copy what they do, and you will also become an expert.

If there is anyone who fits the description of an expert in the field of buying technology products and services, it is Priscilla Tate. Founder of Technology Managers Forum, (www.techforum.com) a professional association that focuses on corporate buying concerns of IT managers in Fortune 1000 companies, Tate has successfully worked at all sides of the IT table. Asked what she considers the most important thing a new IT manager can do when faced with the task of buying a technology product or service, her response is, "Seek out a network of peers who have experience with the product and ask for their opinions."

As simple and logical as that sounds, you would be surprised at how often this good advice is ignored. To their disappointment, many new technology managers quickly and painfully discover how misinforming (mostly through omission) product and service advertising can be.

Tate advises new managers to seek out and join a peer group with a local presence, where they can meet on a regular basis with others doing similar work. She points out that "if you meet with five people who only have five years of experience each, you're tapping in on twenty-five years of experience."

We agree with this completely. Very few new managers seek out and join professional associations upon being newly minted into the management role. Generally, a few years and bloopers later, they decide that they are ready. The fact is that the time to join and get the most out of a professional association is when you are a brand-new manager. As your experience and skills grow, you will continue to draw benefits, as well as contributing to the association. The biggest benefits to you, however, will come when you initially join as a new manager and begin to learn from those who've been in the IT management game much longer than you.

Having access to experienced peers who can help you make an informed decision about products or services is clearly very important. What are some other tools you can use?

Eleven resources from the IT community that can help you

IT is a field that is fortunately rich in available information. You will probably find it more challenging to determine what sources not to use, than to find sources.

The IT Analyst Community consists of companies that specialize in offering you, as the potential buyer, advice on the various types of products and services. Here is a partial list:

Gartner Group — www.gartner.com

Headquartered in Stamford, Connecticut, Gartner helps its clients understand and capitalize on regional market opportunities within a larger global business context. The company boasts unparalleled international capabilities within the research and consulting community, established through 4,300 associates in more than 90 locations worldwide, including Johannesburg, London, New Delhi, Sao Paolo, Sydney, Tel Aviv, and Tokyo.

META Group — www.metagroup.com

META Group is a leading research and consulting firm, focusing on information technology and business transformation strategies. Delivering objective, consistent, and actionable guidance, META Group enables organizations to innovate more rapidly and effectively.

GIGA Information Group — www.gigaweb.com

GIGA is a leading global IT advisory firm providing objective research, pragmatic advice, and personalized consulting. Emphasizing close interaction between analyst and client, GIGA strives to enable you to maximize technology investments and achieve business results.

IDC — www.idc.com

IDC is the world's leading provider of technology intelligence, industry analysis, market data, and strategic and tactical guidance to builders, providers, and users of Information Technology.

Forrester — www.forrester.com

Forrester is a leading independent research firm that analyzes the future of technology change and its impact on businesses, consumers, and society.

The Technology Managers Forum — www.techforum.com

Professional IT management association sites, such as The Technology Managers Forum, focus on providing forums for information exchange between technology providers and IT professionals, particularly where the key focus is on researching corporate buying concerns (your needs).

In addition to the research offered by these sites, you can also benefit from visiting electronic publication sites, such as the following:

CIO Magazine — www.cio.com

An award-winning publication from CXO Media, CIO is geared toward serving the needs of Chief Information Officers and other senior IT executives. This is a good thing to read if you want to follow the advice read by your boss.

Darwin Magazine — www.darwinonline.com

Another product of CXO Media, the focus of Darwin is to provide IT information and insights to business executives, including technology ideas from peers who have had real-life successes and failures. Darwin magazine focuses on using language that is clear, accurate, and straightforward (no techno-jargon).

Information Week — www.informationweek.com

This online magazine includes stories that appear in its printed version, plus daily news, exclusive features, opinion columns, e-mail newsletters, and an interactive community (the Listening Post). Informationweek.com is the site for people who build, buy, invest in, seek to understand, or manage business technology. The published stories provide in-depth analysis, news, research, and perspectives on the latest business technology trends.

Optimize Magazine — www.optimizemag.com

Optimize magazine focuses on providing business technology executives with thought leadership and practical knowledge to bridge the gap between strategy and execution.

Metricnet — www.metricnet.com

If you are looking for benchmark IT financial or operational information, take a look at Metricnet. Founded by META Group EVP Howard Rubin, Metricnet collects data from organizations around the world on IT spending, practices, tools and techniques, staffing, and much more. They then make this data available for download from their site. (Metricnet operates as a "data economy." They basically provide you with downloading "data credits," in return for your providing them with survey data about your IT organization). The data used to prepare the trend reports is collected from a large number of global companies.

Many of the sites listed above offer free newsletters that will keep you informed about changes that might affect you and your company. You can subscribe to these over the Internet in just a few minutes. (Just be judicious, so that you don't end up tripling your daily e-mail diet.)

ACTION ITEMS:

1. Visit the websites listed in this chapter.

2. Find a local IT manager organization and schedule to attend a meeting.

3. Determine which of the listed information sources might best suit your needs as an IT manager.

7

Get Ready, Get Set, Let Go

*Where is the wisdom we have lost in knowledge? Where
is the knowledge we have lost in information?*

T.S. Elliot

Jim — One of the things that I like best about having a coach are the "laser questions" coaches use to get right to the core of the issue. (Yes, I am a coach who has a coach.) One day I was telling my coach, Beth, about some of the new directions my business was taking, and about some of the big projects I was securing. When I finished talking, she said, "So, Jim, what are you letting go of, to make room for these new things you want to do?" Like most people, I was used to just piling on tasks and projects. Beth's question reminded me that every time you say, "yes" to a new task or project, you must say "no" to something else. You can either do this consciously and on purpose, or unconsciously, as your overwhelmed schedule forces you to cut corners or shortchange the things you are doing (often resulting in sub-standard results). That is why it is useful to ask yourself, "By saying 'yes' to doing one thing, what am I saying 'no' to?" This can be a very useful tool to help you become clear about your actions and responsibilities. As a new IT manager, you want to make sure you say "yes" to the things that affect the key responsibilities of your job, which will mean saying "no" to some of the responsibilities of your former job.

Avoid the lose/lose style of work that stresses you while lowering your productivity!

There isn't a human being on the face of the earth who doesn't experience some amount of stress. If you are alive and blood is coursing through your body, you have stress—both good and bad. This is not a chapter about stress management. There are many good books written on this topic, and there is nothing unique about the stress of an IT manager that requires separate or special treatment. What we will focus on here is what you can do to avoid having your current level of stress increased to an inordinate and crippling level by your promotion to IT management. We also want to help you avoid joining the low-productivity busy crowd.

According to a recent Harvard Business Review article entitled "Beware the Busy Manager," only 10% of the managers who took part in the authors' study were involved in activities that moved the company toward its goals. The other 90% were busily involved in unproductive activities that the authors of the article called "active inaction." (The lay term for this is "spinning their wheels.") Unfortunately, a lot of "active inaction" eats up your energy and will leave you feeling not only drained, but frustrated by the low to zero results it produces.

There are at least two things that can drive you toward spurts of overwhelming action that can spike your stress and make you less effective as you enter your new role as an IT manager:

- Taking on the role of IT manager without shedding the tasks of the old role.

- Becoming fretful over your responsibility for the actions of others, and trying to do all the "important work" yourself to make sure it "gets done right."

Let's take a closer look at these and what you can do about them.

Two things you can do to avoid and lower your "new job" stress

Shed the old before taking on the new

One of your worse enemies as you move from one position to another in a company is that old "pack-rat" mentality. We know of people who march into the office every day to face an onslaught of e-mail, much of which has little to do with their current job. How does this happen?

The answer is actually very simple; people are better at collecting information than they are at shedding those things that have lost their usefulness. Go into anyone's attic or garage and we guarantee that you will see evidence of this. Prime real estate, replete with junk that no one ever visits, but which people are afraid to throw out in case they need it one day. Here are some tips for "shedding" the unnecessary items and responsibilities that clutter your life:

- Look at all the e-mail lists you belonged to as part of your old job. Ask to be removed from all lists that are not relevant to your new position.

- Look at your calendar and notice every regular meeting you attended as part of your old job. Find someone to replace you in that meeting, if it is not relevant to your new job.

- Look at your "to do" list. Are you doing only those things that you as the IT manager can do, or are you doing a lot of your old tasks because you are the only one who is involved in these items? Take some of the time you saved by getting out of non-relevant meetings and e-mail lists and use it to train and groom a replacement for those jobs.

- Go through your files and give away or throw away every single piece of paper that does not contain information that is directly relevant to your new position.

Another important time-saver that will keep you focused is advising your team members not to copy you on every piece of correspondence they send out. Tell them that whenever they do copy you, to place a postscript on the note that clearly states the action they want you to take. If they cannot think of an action that you are to take on that specific communication, then there is no reason for you to see it.

To keep you aware of what is going on with the team in terms of their progress and needs, have a regular discussion with them as individuals and/or as a group. This is much better than being copied on every e-mail, which only serves to overwhelm you and keep you from key activities and information that require your attention and focus.

Joe – I have a good friend who is a manager in a global service company. He recently told me that he earmarks any documents that he gets for disposal within six months. I asked him why he did this, and he replied, "In the past I didn't do that, and I became the archive keeper. By making sure that people know I throw everything out in six months, I encourage them to either store it themselves, or know that it is gone. Now I don't waste hours looking for stuff that other people should have if it's really important to them." Sound advice. I started practicing it immediately.

Lose your fretfulness over your responsibility for the actions of others

For most doers in the field of technology, the stress they feel is focused on their performance—what they are currently working on and how well they get it done. Over time, like the players on a baseball team, they become accustomed to the spotlight and scoreboard. However, when you become an IT manager, you are responsible for what other people do. You are also responsible for developing people and making sure that they are effective performers. It is clear that you as the manager, with these responsibilities, will be held accountable by your senior management for the quality of work and level of productivity of your team. As a result, you will begin experiencing a new type of stress.

Many new IT managers react to this stress by micromanaging their team members, or out-and-out taking over the performance of what they consider sensitive tasks in an attempt to control everything and minimize any opportunity for things to go wrong. This is a management formula for disaster, because as you micromanage or put yourself back into a doer role, you become an impediment to your own productivity, and to the productivity of the people you work with.

So, to cope with this new stress, try some of the solutions and ideas listed here:

- Focus your attention on defining what you want done, not how you want your team to do it. Describe the results you want, and constantly ask your team members for their ideas on how you can help them to be successful. Avoid telling people exactly how you want them to handle a job. Your team members will have more personal involvement in projects if they own the solutions/ideas being used, and you will know that your team members are committed.

- Become a teacher and coach. Continually teach and train your people. As they acquire new skills, you will gain their loyalty and can rest assured knowing that the people you have doing a job are highly qualified.

- Create rewards that ensure performance. Make sure that your rewards are in sync with the needs and values of the team. Your team members will then have even more motivation to strive for success.

- Build team communication. Encourage team members to recognize each other's talents and to work together horizontally. This keeps you from always being caught in the middle.

If you devote your efforts to getting results through your team, and to developing their ability to perform, you will find your job will become easier over time.

In addition to these steps, we also recommend that you take a few simple steps to keep the other stressors in your life in check as you acclimate to your new role. Change, even the welcome change of a desired promotion, is always a stress increaser. With this in mind, it is a good idea to take steps to decrease all the other stress producers during your transition to your new role.

Five things you can do to lower your overall stress level while you acclimate to your new role

Here are five things you can immediately start to do to lower and control your stress:

1. Lower your caffeine intake – Many people respond to the demands that stress them by using the caffeine in soft drinks and coffee to keep them going. Of course, they eventually feel "wired," which only worsens the problem. One way to lower your stress level is to lower the caffeine in your life. (You may want to do this gradually, because detoxifying from caffeine can initially cause headaches and some physical discomfort.) If you cannot fully decaffeinate, make an effort not to increase your caffeine consumption in reaction to the new demands.

2. Practice improving your breathing – This may sound overly simple, but it's amazing how many people do not breathe properly. Noted medical expert Andrew Weil has said that if he had only enough time to teach a patient one thing that would have a significant effect on their overall health, he would teach them to breathe properly.

Most people have a very shallow breathing pattern. Interestingly, experts find that this can add to our everyday stress. (I'm sure you've noticed that when you become anxious, you tend to take short, rapid breaths.) One way to relax the pressure is to purposefully slow and deepen your breathing. Below is a three-step breathing technique which is very useful for increasing energy levels and lowering stress. This technique is pretty simple. (It comes from a yoga breathing exercise.) When you are doing this, please remember not to strain at any time, and to stop if you feel dizzy or light-headed. It is not necessary to strain when doing this technique for it to produce results. Regular, sustained practice, will benefit you more over time than trying to master this in your first session. Here are the three steps:

(Note: If you are under the care of a medical practitioner, please consult with him/her before undertaking this or any other physical exercise.)

Inhale for a count of five or six (if this is too much, use a shorter count).

Hold the breath for a count equal to the inhale count (in this example, a count of five).

Exhale for a count equal to twice the inhale count (in this example, using five as your inhale, you would exhale for a count of ten).

You should do this comfortably and without strain. If the numbers above feel too strenuous, use a lower number for the inhale count, and just remember to maintain the 1, 1, 2 ratio for inhale, hold, and exhale, respectively. By practicing this exercise two to three times a day, for five to ten repetitions, you will begin to feel the stress-lowering results in a short time.

3. Exercise regularly – Physical exercise is also one of the best ways to reduce your stress and bring your body back into balance. You don't need to join a health club or buy expensive equipment. Simply walking thirty minutes a day goes a long way toward stress management.

4. Temper your reactions – It has been said that what happens to us is not nearly as important as how we react to what happens. To minimize this effect, in a stressful situation, ask yourself, "How important will this be in ten years?" Also, avoid using some of the common exaggerations used today, such as "I'm totally swamped," to describe having a lot of work to do. Use simple, fact-based descriptions, such as "I have a lot of work to do." This will help put and keep the situation in perspective.

5. Learn to go with the flow of life – I once heard someone say that the last thing they let go of had claw marks on it! Letting go seems to be a big lesson for many of us. We somehow develop a fear of simply allowing life to happen. We create a lot of our frustration by trying to control the outcome of future events. It is important for us to clearly define what we want for ourselves, and to take action toward our goals. You will find this to be a much more fun and less stressful way to live.

By putting into practice the advice in this chapter, you will go a long way toward becoming a more stress-free, purposeful, and focused manager, who produces value-adding results.

ACTION ITEMS:

1. Take a look at your calendar, to-do list, and e-mails, and create a list of things you will eliminate in order to make room for the new activities you must engage in as an IT manager.

2. Take another look at your activities, and target for delegation any doer activities that you will no longer personally do as a manager. (Remember to slot in time to communicate, coach, and train the person to whom you delegate these assignments.)

3. Pick at least two of the stress-lowering activities in the list of five at the end of this chapter and commit to practicing them for thirty days. (We believe you will be delighted with the results and encouraged to do more.)

8

DEALING WITH A CURVE BALL:
OUTSOURCING

*Turbulence is life force. It is opportunity. Let's love turbulence
and use it for change.*

RAMSAY CLARK

What is outsourcing and why do you need to understand it?

This chapter covers a topic that you may or may not have to deal with in the future. Nevertheless, it is an important topic, as many companies today may choose to outsource the function you manage.

Outsourcing is a strategic partnership, in which a company like yours entrusts a supplier with the responsibility for handling a specific process. For example, if a company hires a supplier to handle their IT Help Desk, it becomes the supplier's responsibility to make investments in tools and training to provide a contracted quality of service. Your company, as the customer, pays the supplier to maintain a level of service quality defined in a service level agreement or statement of work. (The agreement, for example, might specify that a technician must be dispatched within a certain number of hours after a call, if that call cannot be handled at the Help Desk.)

If your function were to be outsourced, the team that is now reporting to you could very likely end up becoming members of the supplier company. Reading this, we are sure your first question is, "What about me? If the team reports to the outsourcing supplier, does my job go away?" The answer, as you will see, is that you can actually benefit from this arrangement in a few ways, by just taking a creative approach.

Why do companies outsource?

One of the reasons that companies outsource is to focus less time, attention, and investment on those functions that are not core to their business. If you did the Alignment Charting exercise, as well as the IT Investment Portfolio exercise, and found that the area you manage is in the Run-the-Business portfolio, you may be managing a candidate for outsourcing.

According to Peter Bendor-Samuel, a world expert on outsourcing, organizations realize that they "cannot be excellent at delivering all of the IT services their companies require. In fact, the more prudent course is to strive to be good at non-core functions, but not excellent. To be excellent in every aspect of IT would require making tremendous amounts of investments. Let's face it, there are some things where you don't really need to be excellent." In many cases, Bendor-Samuel adds, "Supplier companies can provide the same or a better quality of service to your company, due to having leverage." What Bendor-Samuel refers to as "leverage" are things such as an infrastructure that can be shared across multiple clients, or any other resources that enable the supplier to handle the work at a lower cost.

The bottom line is that in most instances, you cannot make a strong business case for not outsourcing a function that has been earmarked for "farming-out." So what are some of the things that an IT manager needs to know about outsourcing? First of all, you need to know that while outsourcing tends to scare people within IT organizations, it doesn't necessarily need to scare you. More importantly, you should not set yourself to oppose it.

Bendor-Samuel advises, "Do not throw your body in front of outsourcing." Furthermore, he adds, "If you are a better miler or sprinter, you might be able to turn an outsourcing engagement into a career opportunity for yourself, either with the supplier company or by becoming the enabler—the person who leverages your company's decision to outsource."

Here are some of the things you can do to benefit yourself, your team, and your company if the company decides to outsource your function:

- Be a change facilitator for your team.
- Become the outsourcer's liaison to your company.
- If you can't beat them, join them.

Let's take a close look at each one of these.

Three things you can do to benefit from your company's decision to outsource

1. Be a change facilitator for your team

If your company is outsourcing, some of the people who are now reporting to you will be afraid of being shunted over to a "strange and unknown" supplier company, or worse yet, losing their jobs. Your company is probably very concerned about this, and with good reason. Many companies lose key employees when they announce the decision to outsource. This loss can be very painful, leaving the company without vital talent and experience during a major transition period. Also, many of the people who leave may enter lateral positions, just to get away from what they see as a dangerous situation.

Here are a few steps you can take to facilitate the transition and minimize the impact on people and the company, while playing a vital role that will not go unnoticed by your company.

- Get as much information as you can from your management about the upcoming outsourcing deal and the supplier company. Also, open communications with a Human Resources professional who is knowledgeable in outsourcing transitions. Have this individual join you in meetings with your team, in order to discuss the deal and answer questions. Some of the things the team will want to know about are any changes in compensation, benefit packages, and/or other fringe benefits. If the supplier offers better career opportunities (and they often do), tell the team. Handle any emotional spikes with considerate understanding. Even when faced with the prospect of a better deal, most people do not like changes that are brought upon them by outside circumstances.

- Encourage team members to bring any questions that come up to you. Promptly seek answers and reply to those questions.

- Get the managers of the supplier company in front of the team as soon as possible. People tend to fear the actions of unknown faces much more than they do the actions of people they've met.

- Do not expect immediate acceptance. Change is a process, not unlike grieving. The person making the change must first totally accept the burial of the past, before they can embrace the present and the future. This will not happen overnight.

By acting as the "change agent" and facilitator for your team, you will be showing great leadership and maturity and playing a vital role for your company, the supplier company, and your team. This will open up more options for you as your company completes the transition into the new relationship with the outsourcer. Here are the two key options:

- You can become the outsourcer's liaison on behalf of your company.
- You can join the outsourcer's company and become the outsourcer's team manager, stationed on site at your former company.

Let's take a closer look at these.

2. Become the outsourcer's liaison on behalf of your company

Many companies place the former manager of an IT function in this role when they outsource. The company views this as a good match, since you (as the former manager of the internal function) know the needs of the clients using the service, and can provide useful input to the supplier.

Before you accept this position, we ask that you go back to the beginning of this book and do another exercise designed to answer the question, "Is being the Outsourcing Relationship Manager the right role for me?" Remember, as your company's Outsourcing Relationship Manager with the supplier, your job will no longer be to manage the delivery of the products or services provided by the outsourced function. In your new role, you will be the person who interfaces with the supplier's management team charged with running the operation. Your role will be to find ways to help the supplier provide your company with the best value. In our initial analogy in the opening chapters of this book, we compared the team member with the pitcher on a baseball team and the manager with the coach. As the Outsourcing Relationship Manager, you must relinquish your role as the coach to the supplier's management team, and adopt the role of "owner." If this is not the role for you, decline it. If it is the right role for you, read on and learn how to make the most of it.

How to become a highly valued liaison between your company and the outsourcer

Bendor-Samuel tells us that there are two types of Outsourcing Relationship Managers: the "Problem-Finders," who are destructive, and the "Solution-Leveragers," who are constructive.

"Problem-Finders" seek total contract compliance, and view anything short of complete attainment (even beyond reasonable expectations) as failure. Upon finding these failures, they proceed to pummel the supplier toward total compliance. The problem with the "Problem-Finders" is that they nickel and dime the supplier so much, they often create a hostile relationship in which each party views the other as the enemy. In this win/lose, high pressure relationship, suppliers do the least they must, "Problem-Finders" get ulcers, and the company gets a lot less than they could. Many "Problem-Finders" are motivated by the belief that they are the real experts in serving the people who consume the service. Generally, they are insecure about their jobs, and get in the way of the supplier. Often, after a few suppliers have left and the company begins to notice the common denominator, the "Problem-Finders" make their own fears come true. (They get fired.)

> **Joe** — I knew an IT manager who was such an adamant "Problem-Finder" that he forbade the management of the supplier to take action on any problem until they cleared it with him. The results were disastrous, with multiple delays and other service lags. For years, this "Problem-Finder" got away with blaming the suppliers. A new senior management team, however, came into power, and they didn't buy it. They terminated the "Problem-Finder," put another Relationship Manager in place, and all the problems disappeared; end-user satisfaction soared and expenses dropped. "Solution-Leveragers," on the other hand, are quite the opposite of "Problem-Finders." "Solution-Leveragers," according to

Bendor-Samuel, seek to understand the full capabilities of the supplier, and then discover ways to drive more value to their company by further engaging the supplier's services.

For example, a "Solution-Leverager," upon hearing of a large relocation project, will ask the management of their Help Desk supplier to discuss what they offer to handle relocations. Or they may discover that there is a separate customer support center for applications in another part of the company, and ask the supplier to discuss how they might expand their umbrella to cover those services at a cost savings to the company.

The role of the "Solution-Leverager" is certainly a more positive, valuable, and mutually rewarding one. By seeking out ways the supplier can bring even more savings to the company, which represents added revenue to the supplier, the "Solution-Leverager" is a creative force in the business of finding win/win situations.

3. If you can't beat them, join them

Finally, another option, as noted above, is to join the supplier's company and continue to be the manager of the team delivering the service to your company (now your client company). This is an especially good choice if a re-examination of your career direction reveals that you do not want to be the Outsourcing Relationship Manager, but are better suited for the role of the process manager.

Moving into the supplier's organization may actually be a great career move for you. For one thing, the function that was outsourced by your previous company as a "Run-the-Business" service is clearly one of the core services of the supplier company. The supplier company will likely have a longer and more lucrative set of career track options for someone with your background.

> **Joe** – It is not uncommon in technology companies for technical professionals and entry-level managers to work their way up the ladder to more senior management positions, as well as more senior technical roles. In the sixteen years of my career on the client side, I found this to be an extremely rare occurrence. Clearly, companies that are in the business of supplying

IT services have more opportunities for people in the IT profession. As the old saying goes, "It is always better to work in a company that is in your chosen field of business."

The Employee Lifecycle© HR Model was therefore created to map out a strategy for addressing this new frontier. For those of you interested in having a fuller understanding of this model, below is a full reprint of the paper that defines the basis for and structure of this new model, reprinted with full permission of its author, Dr. Jon Couture.

Closing thoughts on outsourcing

Outsourcing is not something that you are going to run into a lot within the span of your career. You may encounter it once, maybe twice. Peter Bendor-Samuel says, "outsourcing is like getting married. It is a long-term reciprocal partnership between a company and a supplier who are in it for the long haul."

This being the case, you don't really need to develop a lot of expertise in outsourcing. You simply need to recognize it and know a little bit about how to address it if and when it comes up in your career path.

ACTION ITEM:

To become more familiar with outsourcing, in terms of the types of functions outsourced and the latest trends, visit the Outsourcing Journal at www.outsourcing-journal.com.

9

BONUS CHAPTER
THE EMPLOYEE LIFECYCLE© HR MODEL

In the parlance of the Employee Lifecycle© HR Model, all the preceding chapters in this book were designed to address the need for Orientation and Socialization of an employee undergoing a role change. The phenomenon of people experiencing a frequent need for re-orientation and socialization within a career with one company is a relatively new outgrowth of our high-pace, ever-changing business world. Unlike the world of just two decades ago, when an employee who had been with a company for thirty years had perhaps not held more than two or three jobs, today, someone with six years experience in one company may have already held four different roles.

The Employee Lifecycle© HR Model was therefore created to map out a strategy for addressing this new frontier. For those of you interested in having a fuller understanding of this model, below is a full reprint of the paper that defines the basis for and structure of this new model, reprinted with full permission of its author, Dr. Jon Couture, Senior Vice President of Human Resources, Siemens Business Services.

The Employee Lifecycle© HR Model

While human resources practices have existed since the advent of organized work, the actual field of human resources in America dates back to 1786 when the first employee strike took place (Sherman, Bohlander & Chruden, 1988). Initially titled 'personnel', the focus of this field dealt primarily with policies and procedures, employee discipline issues and the labor relations aspect of operating a business successfully.

As modern countries actively engaged in the industrial boom of the 19th century the need for more sophisticated human resources practices became evident. Job functions became increasingly more complex, labor unions were formed to drive minimum standards for factory working conditions and managing employees became more sophisticated. The need for a more sophisticated approach to human resources (HR) management was clear. As the world of business became more complex, HR practices followed this trend. Examples of this include increasingly specific labor laws (e.g., Equal Employment Opportunity, Occupational Safety and Health Act, etc.) and more focused HR practices (e.g., recruiting techniques, job training, organizational development, etc.).

While the advancements in the HR field have been significant, the advent of the 'information age' is forcing HR professionals to approach the various disciplines within HR more systematically than ever. There is clearly a need for a theoretical model that shows the relationships between the major functional areas within the HR field. This paper introduces a 'lifecycle' approach to HR management.

Origins of the Employee Lifecycle© HR Model

The Employee Lifecycle© HR model was created out of necessity. In today's fast moving business environments, managers are under a great deal of pressure to develop high performance teams. As they work to achieve this goal, there is a tendency to request high-end HR services (e.g., employee development, succession planning) before other, more basic issues are taken care of (e.g., basic employee awareness, compensation and benefits issues, etc.). In a sense, this situation is analogous to 'putting the cart before the horse'. Unfortunately, when this happens, it results in poor employee performance, managerial frustration and reduced shareholder value due to ineffective HR systems and services.

The Employee Lifecycle© was created as a result of observing a trend in the HR field. This trend showed several failed attempts to improve employee performance and business results through enhanced training and development activities. Companies spent millions of dollars on various training and development initiatives, however, there was little apparent improvement in employee performance. In each case, employees had basic needs that were not being met (e.g., contextual understanding of the work environment, payroll issues, etc.). This lack of attention to lower-order HR issues seemed to cause a significant reduction in the value of the higher-order HR activities. In order to address this systematically, a new HR model would be needed so that HR professionals and business managers could partner to create truly high-performing teams.

The 'cart before the horse' issue mentioned above is common to all industries. The key to understanding why this happens is understanding the interrelationships between the various functional areas within HR and applying a hierarchical model to these functions. Additionally, the various functions within HR are cyclical (i.e., the inputs to the model are the same as the outputs). Finally, there are several iterative processes (e.g., communications, performance management) that facilitate the smooth transition from one component of the model to another. The next section describes the major research that supports the Employee Lifecycle© HR model.

Components of the Employee Lifecycle© HR Model

The Employee Lifecycle© HR model consists of five primary components and three supporting components. The following list outlines the components in each category:

1. Primary Components

Recruiting

Orientation/socialization

Job performance

Employee development

Succession planning

Supporting Components

Communications

Performance management

Teaching

It's important to note that the model applies to new and existing employees (hence the differentiation between recruiting [new] and staffing [existing] as the inputs to the model). Additionally, the supporting components work in an iterative fashion thus ensuring two-way feedback exists throughout the various functions. This creates a check-and-balance system so managers have a means of understanding where to focus their time relative to the employee's needs. The following sections provide additional details on each component within the Employee Lifecycle© model.

Recruiting/Staffing

The first HR function of the employment process is recruiting. This function deals with all aspects of bringing a new employee on board in a new company. Examples of the subfunctions within recruiting include: employee requisitioning, employment advertising, resume collection, candidate tracking, offer letter generation and pre-employment logistics (e.g., filling out an application).

An interesting element of the recruiting/staffing function is that it acts as both the inputs and outputs to the Employee Lifecycle© model. Once an employee moves through the various components of the model, (s)he will ultimately work with the recruiting/staffing team on finding the next position within the company (e.g., a promotion). It's important to understand that once an employee changes positions within the company, the manager must reinitiate the Employee Lifecycle© processes to ensure the employee is optimally equipped for success in his/her new position. Figure 2 shows how the process works.

Figure 2., Employee career progression shows how Employee Lifecycle© model continuously cycles

Once a new or existing employee is settled in his/her new position, a transition occurs to the orientation/socialization phase of the Employee Lifecycle© process. The next section describes the key activities in this phase.

Orientation/Socialization

When an employee starts in a new position, it's critical to

ensure (s)he is properly socialized into his/her new environment. The research in this area is clear: employee orientation/socialization has been linked to employee productivity (Schein, 1979). There are three major stages of employee orientation:

Pre-start

Rapid onboarding

Post-start follow-up

In the pre-start stage, final details associated with the employee's job offer are closed and (s)he is given a set of new hire paperwork to complete prior to the first day of employment. Additionally, the new employee's manager works through various logistical issues (e.g., procuring a computer, office supplies, access keys, etc.) to ensure the employee is maximally productive on his/her first day at work.

Once an employee starts working, a rapid onboarding process begins. This process includes taking care of various administrative duties (e.g., setting up payroll, selecting health benefits, etc.), getting introduced to coworkers and familiarization with the new work environment. This stage also includes various 'orientation' programs that are designed to get the new employee familiar with local, national and global aspects of the new organization. It is the joint responsibility of the employee and his/her manager to ensure these things happen on a timely basis.

The final stage of the orientation/socialization process is post-start follow up. This stage is designed to be an open dialog between an employee and a manager in terms of ensuring all logistical and social aspects of the job are taken care of. This stage should be viewed as a feedback loop for the employee so that no basic need (e.g., connectivity to the company intranet) goes unmet. The last part of this stage is a 90-day performance review. This is designed to ensure the employee is clear about his/her role, is meeting the expectations of his/her manager and any developmental needs are identified and a training plan is put into place to address the developmental issues. The next component of the

Employee Lifecycle© model deals with various HR systems and will be covered in the next section.

HR Systems Stability

Once an employee is properly oriented/socialized into his/her new work environment, it's important to ensure various HR systems, processes and procedures accurately reflect the employee's status. The following list outlines several key HR systems that must be initiated and maintained over the employee's tenure with the company:

HR information accuracy – This information is the basis of an employee's record of employment. It is the warehouse for all personnel information (job grade, address, work location, compensation, benefits selections, etc.). If this information is not accurate, it can have a major negative impact on employee productivity because employees will generally focus on resolving issues associated with inaccurate records (e.g., wrong payroll information) before being able to fully focus on work tasks.

Benefits – Another critical basic need for an employee is ensuring his/her health and welfare benefits are accurate. When the need arises to use a given benefit (e.g., the employee's spouse or child needs to go to the doctor) it's important that everything is in order (e.g., the proper level of coverage is in place) or the employee will be distracted from his/her work if an issue arises that needs to be addressed.

Compliance – There are certain legal and/or company requirements that apply to every employee. Examples of this include safety and health rules and regulations, company policies and procedures and, in some cases, customer requirements.

The basic theme associated with this component of the Employee Lifecycle© model is distraction minimization. It is important for managers to work hard to address all of an employee's basic needs so (s)he can focus of his/her work. The next section addresses the details associated with ensuring an employee is properly equipped to perform his/her job.

	Stimulus	Response	Consequences
Environmental	**Information** 1. description of what is expected of performance 2. Clear and relevant guides on how to do the job 3. Relevant and frequent feedback on adequacy of performance	**Resources** 4. Tools, resources, time and materials designed to achieve performance needs 5. Access to leaders 6. Sufficient personnel 7. organized work processes	**Incentives** 8. Adequate financial incentives contingent upon performance 9. Non-monetary incentives 10. Career development opportunities 11. Clear consequences for poor performance
Personal	**Knowledge** 12. Systematically designed training to match requirements of exemplary performers 13. Opportunity for training	**Capacity** 14. Match between people and position 15. Good selection processes 16. Flexible scheduling to match capacity workers. 17. Prosthesis or visual aids to augment capacity	**Motivation** 18. Recognition of worker's willingness to work for available incentives 19. Assessment of worker's motivation 20. Recruitment of workers to match realities of work conditions

Job Performance

The job performance component of the Employee Lifecycle[©] HR model is the nucleus of this model. Once an employee has been properly socialized into a new work environment and his/her HR systems are stable, the entire focus of a manager's efforts should shift to address the employee's needs in terms of job specific skills, knowledge and tools. Specifically, this component consists of addressing the environmental and personal needs of the employee to ensure (s)he is properly equipped to perform a given job in an efficient and effective manner. Gilbert (1978) created a behavioral engineering model that outlines six critical aspects of the job performance component of the Employee Lifecycle[©] HR model. The figure below outlines the six areas of Gilbert's model.

Each element of this model can be applied to an employee's position. The outcome of this application is that an employee clearly understands his/her role, is properly equipped to perform his/her assigned tasks, is fairly compensated and is properly motivated. Once these aspects are taken care of, the manager can begin focusing on further developing the employee's skills and experiences through formal employee development. The next section discusses this topic.

Employee Development

A key part of retaining good employees is having a specific plan developed that shows an employee his/her progression in a given organization. Every employee development process assumes that the employee is performing at an acceptable level in his/her existing job. In general terms, a training and development plan is established for an employee after ninety days of employment. The purpose of this plan is twofold: 1) ensure the requisite skills and knowledge for a given job are maintained and 2) prepare the employee for his/her next assignment in the organization. The following are the basic components of an employee development plan:

Key accountabilities – the measurable objectives an employee is expected to perform within a given period of time (typically one year).

Performance goals – the long term objectives an employee is supposed to achieve in order to advance to the next level in his/her career.

Training plan – a specific set of learning activities targeted at providing the employee with advanced knowledge in his/her existing role or introductory knowledge at the next level of career advancement. Training should be targeted in the technical, business and interpersonal skill areas.

Experience plan – a documented approach to job rotation that ensures the employee has exposure to the necessary experiences for performing advanced duties (typically associated with the next level of career progression within a given job).

Periodic feedback – this step in the process ensures that the employee receives performance feedback on a periodic basis so as to stay on track with the plan (s)he developed with his/her manager.

Another form of employee development is succession planning. The key difference between employee development and succession planning is that the company typically drives the succession planning process (as opposed to the employee driving the process). The next section describes the succession planning process in more detail.

Succession Planning

In order for companies to be prepared for changes in their markets (e.g., expanding into a new industry) and personnel (e.g., the sudden resignation of a key manager) succession planning processes must be developed as far down into the organization as possible. This component of the Employee Lifecycle© HR model is a systematic approach for identifying and developing high-potential employees and managers. The following steps outline the succession planning process. A brief explanation is provided following each step.

Development of leadership competency models – The first step in the succession planning process is defining the key competencies associated with exemplary leaders in a given organization. This model will be different for each organization.

Organizational assessment against the competency models – Typically called 'stack ranking', this process is an objective evaluation of each member in a given organization that results in a rank order of each member. Employees generally do a self-evaluation which is compared to the manager's evaluation. The gaps between the employee and manager evaluations are reviewed and discussed. Normally the top 5%-10% of the employees participating in this process are considered 'high potentials' and are included in the succession planning process.

Creation of development plans to address skill and experience gaps identified during the organizational assessment – Specific plans are developed that guide an employee or manager through various training courses and experiences that close the gaps identified during the organizational assessment process.

Mentoring and coaching of high-potential employees and managers – Once high-potential employees have been identified, a mentor or sponsor is assigned to the employee so (s)he can have an experienced, senior representative of the company to work with (and seek counsel from) as the development takes place.

Periodic review of succession plans by leadership team – Succession plans are periodically reviewed in an annual or semi-annual process that looks at all of the succession plans across the enterprise. Typically, this occurs at the Director level and above.

The succession planning process results in qualified candidates for promotion into lateral or higher level positions within the company. As Figure 1 shows above, the succession planning process feeds the recruiting/staffing organization and the Employee Lifecycle© process starts over at orientation. The next section describes the iterative processes that run in parallel with the hierarchical phases of the model.

Iterative Processes

In order to ensure the Employee Lifecycle© HR model operates smoothly, several iterative processes must happen in concert with the activities associated with each major component of the model. There are three major categories that comprise the iterative processes: 1) Communication, 2) Performance Management and 3)Teaching. The following paragraphs provide a brief summary of each of these processes:

Communications – A critical success factor to any activity within the employee/manager relationship is the degree to which the parties communicate. Given the advent of the remote worker (e.g., telecommuting), managers must work hard to communicate with their employees frequently and through various media (e.g., email, telephone, in person, video conferencing, etc.). Managers who have good communications with their employees are able to head-off many problems before they grow in severity and complexity.

Performance Management – This process provides a systematic approach for goal setting and progress monitoring. Most managers use this process as a mechanism for expectation management so that employees can understand how they are performing against agreed upon goals. Conversely, employees typically use this process as a means of managing their workload (i.e., when a manager asks the employee to take on additional responsibilities the employee has an objective basis by which to negotiate the extra work.).

Teaching – Toward the middle of the 1990s, many prominent management consultants espoused a concept called 'the learning organization'(Senge, 1994). The key concept in Senge's work focuses on the notion that employees and managers must perpetually learn in order to survive in the business world of the future. As the 1990s drew to a close, the Internet economy had grown exponentially and the 'learning organization' concept evolved into the 'teaching organization' (Tichy, 1997). The basic premise of the teaching organization is that it's every manager's job to not only learn perpetually but to share the information they learn with their teams. By doing this, organizations capture and distribute knowledge more effectively, thus resulting in improved operational effectiveness and efficiency.

Each of the iterative processes occur simultaneously and constantly. They act as the oil that allows the components of the Employee Lifecycle© HR model to work together, as well as the glue that holds the model together. The next section explains the relationships between the components of the model.

Interrelationships Between Employee Lifecycle© Components

There are three distinct relationships between the components of the Employee Lifecycle© HR model; 1) linearity, 2) continuous loop and 3) interaction of the iterative processes. As described in the previous section, the major components of the model are hierarchical and linear. The Employee Lifecycle© theory suggests that employees will focus on the component that has the greatest degree of need for attention (i.e., an unsatisfied need); much like Maslow's hierarchy of needs (1948). The hierarchical nature of the interaction between the major components of the model necessitates a linear relationship as well.

Once an employee has cycled through each of the components of the Employee Lifecycle© HR model, the recruiting organization acts as a conduit for placing the employee in his/her next position. Ideally, the employee would continue to cycle through all aspects of the model for the entirety of the employee's working years (although, given the current dynamics in the labor market, this is unlikely).

Finally, the iterative processes are always in action, regardless of where the employee is on the hierarchy. They provide a support sub-system for the rest of the model and are critical to the ongoing and effective operation of the model.

Research and/or Theories that support the Employee Lifecycle© HR Model

The key literature that provides the basis for the Employee Lifecycle© HR Model is found in the areas of human resources planning, employee orientation, training and development and motivation. The following areas provide additional information on these topics.

In order for businesses to meet their strategic objectives, it's important to integrate the human resources plan with the business strategy (Kaufman, 1984). Galosy (1983) did a study on the effects of having a systematic approach to human resources planning and found an increase in business performance within organizations that implemented a systematic human resources plan that aligned with the business plan.

Once the human resources plan is created, the human resources team works with line managers to recruit, onboard, train and develop employees through their tenure at a given company. There is a fair amount of research that supports the need for properly orienting new employees (Hiatt, 1983; Pascale, 1984; Truell, 1981 and Reed-Mendenhall & Milliard, 1980). Each of these studies sites the value of orientation in terms of reducing employee turnover and increasing productivity.

There is also a significant amount of literature that documents the value of systematically approaching job design (Levine, Ash, Hall and Sistrunk, 1983) and training (Smith, 1980). Additionally, the literature clearly shows the value of various career development models (Walker & Gutteridge, 1979, Moravec, 1982, Holland, 1984).

Probably the most influential theory on the Employee Lifecycle© HR model is Maslow's hierarchy of needs. Maslow (1954) attempted to synthesize the large body of research on human motivation by creating a hierarchical model that explained how humans cannot develop advanced needs (e.g., belonging) until their lower-level needs are met (e.g., food and shelter). This concept can be directly applied to the various functions within an organization as it relates to meeting the basic and advanced needs of employees.

This section outlined some of literature that supports the Employee Lifecycle© theory. The next section provides a critical analysis of the implications of this model.

Critical analysis of the Employee Lifecycle©

The Employee Lifecycle© HR model is a framework for aligning the various human resources functions within a given company to the needs of the business. Additionally, this model acts as a blueprint for where human resources professionals should focus their attention (e.g., focus on lower-level activities before higher-level activities). While the model itself is unique, the components of the model are not. The benefit of synthesizing this information into a model is that it allows organizations to focus scarce resources on the right priorities. The Employee Lifecycle© theory claims that companies waste millions of dollars on various human resources activities (team building training, technical training, etc.) when more basic employee needs (e.g., orientation) have not been met.

The results of not systematically addressing employees' human resources needs are lower productivity, increased employee turnover and managerial confusion.

If there is an area where the Employee Lifecycle© HR model is lacking it would be in empirical support. Since this is a novel model, there is no research that supports (or rejects) the hierarchical relationship proposed by the theory. Additionally, it's possible that the model can be consolidated to simplify its presentation. An example of this would be to consolidate the Orientation and HR Systems components into one component. A good argument can also be made for consolidating the Employee Development and Succession Planning components into one component. The rationale for this is that both employee development and succession planning are career development methods and it might make sense to view the upper portion of the model in this way.

As it currently exists, the model is fairly self-explanatory. While consolidating components would make the model simpler, it might detract from the differentiation that exists between the components and the tools, processes and procedures unique to a given component (e.g., stack ranking as it relates to succession planning). In this sense, it would be helpful for future research on this model to determine whether or not consolidation makes sense.

Summary and Conclusions

In summary, this paper proposed a new human resource management model that is based on Maslow's (1954) hierarchy of needs theory. In the age of the Internet, all companies need to make sure they systematically approach the human resources needs of their employees. The Employee Lifecycle© HR model is a blueprint for setting up and maintaining all aspects of a modern human resources organization to address the changing needs of employees at all levels. Properly implemented, the Employee Lifecycle© HR model can improve employee productivity and satisfaction while reducing employee turnover to below industry standard levels.

REFERENCES

Galosy, J.R. (year?). Meshing Human Resources Planning with Strategic Business Planning: One Company's Experience. Personnel, Vol. 60, No. 5, pp. 26-35.

Gilbert, T. (1978). Human Competence. New York, McGraw-Hill.

Hiatt, S.R. (1983). The Effects of Social Orientation on Socialization Outcomes of New Nurses in Hospitals. Unpublished dissertation, Arizona State University.

Holland, J.I. (1984). Making Vocational Choices: A Theory of Careers, 2nd Ed. Englewood Cliffs, NJ, Prentice-Hall.

Kaufman, D.J. (1984). Planning: Strategic, Human Resources and Employment: An Integrated Approach. Managerial Planning, Vol. 32, No. 6, pp. 24-27.

Levine, E.L., Ash, R.A., Hall, H., Sistrunk, F. (1983). Evaluation of Job Analysis Methods by Experienced Job Analysts. Academy of Management Journal, Vol. 26, pp. 339-348.

Maslow, A.H. (1948). 'Higher' and 'Lower' Needs. Journal of Psychology, No. 25, pp. 433-436.

Maslow, A.H. (1954). Motivation and Personality. New York, Harper and Brothers.

Moravec, M. (1982). A Cost Effective Career Planning Program Requires a Strategy. Personnel Administrator, Vol. 27, No. 1, pp. 28-32.

Pascale, R. (1984). Fitting New Employees into the Company Culture. Fortune, Vol. 109, No. 11, p. 28.

Reed-Mendenhall, D., Milliard, C.W. (1980). Orientation: A Training and Development Tool. Personnel Administrator, Vol. 25, No. 8, pp. 40-44.

Schein. (1979). Toward a Theory of Organizational Socialization. In Research in Organizational Behavior. Ed. B.M. Staw. Greenwich, CT. JAI Press. 1: 209-264

Senge, P.M., Kleiner, A., Roberts, C., Ross, R.B., Smith, B.J. (1994). The Fifth Discipline Fieldbook. New York, Doubleday.

Sherman, A.W., Bohlander, G.W., Chruden, H.J. (1988). Managing Human Resources. Cincinnati, OH, South-Western Publishing Company.

Smith, M.E. (1980). Evaluating Training Operations and Programs. Training and Development Journal. Vol. 34, No. 10, pp. 70-78.

Tichy, N.M., Cohen, E.B. (1997). The Leadership Engine: How Winning Companies Create Leaders at All Levels. New York, HarperCollins.

Truell, G.F. (1981). Tracking Down the 'Aroundhereisms' – or How to Foil Negative Orientation. Personnel. Vol. 58, No. 4, pp. 23-31.

Walker, J.W., Gutteridge, T.G. (1979). Career Planning Practices, An AMA Survey Report. American Management Association, New York.

ADDITIONAL RESOURCES

Give a man a fish and you feed him for a day. Teach a man to fish and you feed him for a lifetime.

CHINESE PROVERB

Where do we go from here? Well, this is just the beginning of a great start to a great new career. We recommend that you continue to build on the foundation you've started by reading the books listed below.

To help you build your management and leadership capabilities

The One Minute Manager by Spencer Johnson and Ken Blanchard

The One Minute Manager Meets the Monkey by Ken Blanchard and William Oncken, Jr.

Leadership and the One Minute Manager: Increasing Effectiveness with Situational Leadership by Patricia Zigarmi

The Wisdom of Teams: Creating High Performance Organizations by Jon R. Katzenbach and Douglas K. Smith

Leadership Jazz by Max DePree

Get the Best Out of Your People and Yourself by Val Williams

Inspire Any Audience by Tony Jeary

To develop your hiring and interviewing techniques

Coaching for an Extraordinary Life by Terri Levine

Co-Active Coaching by Laura Whitworth, Henry Kimsey-House, and Phil Sandhal

To help you find your personal values and gain focus

Breaking the Rules by Kurt Wright

Reclaim Your Life by Jim Donovan

This is Your Life, Not a Dress Rehearsal by Jim Donovan

Handbook to a Happier life by Jim Donovan

Create a Life that Tickles Your Soul by Suzanne Willis Zoglio, Ph.D.

Power of Focus by Jack Canfield, Mark V. Hansen, and Les Hewitt

To help you cope with stressors

Inforelief, Stay Afloat in the Infoflood by Maureen Malanchuk

Turn-It-Off; How to Unplug from the Anytime-Anywhere Office Without Disconnecting Your Career by Gil Gordon

Work Yourself Happy by Terri Levine

To give you a more in-depth view of outsourcing

Turning Lead Into Gold; The Demystification of Outsourcing by Peter Bendor-Samuel

PARTING WORDS

Every contrivance of man, every tool, every instrument, every utensil, every article designed for use, of each and every kind, evolved from a very simple beginning.

ROBERT COLLIER

Congratulations on your promotion and on taking the first step to becoming a successful IT manager. We encourage you to keep this book nearby and refer to it again from time to time for ideas you can use to enhance your management capabilities.

As you begin your new career, remember to give yourself time for your skills to evolve. Your decision to pursue an IT management career after careful personal assessment, as well as your dedication to building a sound foundation as demonstrated by your reading this book, is evidence that you have "the right stuff." We are confident that with time and practice you will do a great job, which may lead to finding yourself joyfully faced with more and ever-growing career choices.

We would love to know how the strategies presented in this book have worked for you. Please send your success stories to our publisher at itbookstories@lahaskapublishing.com.

We wish you the best of success!

Joe Santana & Jim Donovan

ABOUT THE AUTHORS

JOE SANTANA

Joe Santana is a Director in a leading global technology outsourcing and consulting services company. He has twenty-one years of experience as an IT executive.

Joe has been referred to as having a 360° view of the IT world as a result of having roles that included buying, selling, and leading enterprise IT delivery teams in fast-paced business environments.

Joe has also taught and coached hundreds of new IT managers and IT sales representatives, and has often been quoted in well-known industry and business publications regarding key IT topics including Fortune Magazine and the Outsourcing Journal.

Joe's articles have been published to a broad range of audiences in numerous trade and professional publications. He is a frequent guest on business radio and network television.

His previous published works include co-authoring a popular Internet marketing audiocassette program entitled *Internet Gold: The Basics* published by Pharaoh Audiobooks in 1995.

JIM DONOVAN

For more than 25 years, Jim Donovan has worked with individuals, companies, and organizations to implement strategies for personal and professional growth.

Jim is a frequent speaker to businesses, trade groups, and associations, and his seminars have benefited hundreds of audiences nationwide. His seminars inspire individuals to take charge of their lives, provide them with transformational ideas and strategies for their success, and inspire them to achieve peak performance.

Jims coaching programs employ a proven step-by-step process that synthesizes some of the most effective information, tools and methods from the fields of marketing, sales, quantum physics and universal spirituality. They are uniquely designed to identify the strengths within an organization and build upon them. His focus is on helping clients produce significant, explosive results and quantum leaps well beyond what is expected.

As an internationally recognized author, his books have been translated into four languages and distributed worldwide, including his bestseller, *Handbook To A Happier Life*, a simple guide to creating the life you've always wanted, *This Is Your Life, Not A Dress Rehearsal*, proven principles for creating the life of your dreams, and *Reclaim Your Life*, how to regain your happiness through challenging times.

Since 1991, he has published an internationally syndicated newsletter for personal and professional development, aimed at business executives, entrepreneurs, and individuals. Jim is a popular guest on radio talk shows and TV stations, and a regular member of the "brain trust" for The Small Business Advocate syndicated radio show. His articles regularly appear in newspapers and magazines as well as on the Internet.

TO LEARN MORE:

For information about additional products for I.T. Managers, special reports, free downloadable forms, seminars, Web casts, audio products, and more, visit **www.manageitbook.com**

For information about our I.T. Management and organizational coaching programs, please visit **www.bentleypartnership.com**

ORDERING INFORMATION

Individual copies can be ordered at
www.manageitbook.com

or on Amazon.com, bn.com and in traditional bookstores.

Manage I.T. is available at special quantity discounts for bulk purchases for *sales promotions, premiums, fund-raising, or educational use.*

Special books or book excerpts can be created to fit specific needs.

Call Lahaska Publishing (215) 794–3826 for details on bulk quantity purchases or email maria@lahaskapublishing.com or write Lahaska Publishing, PO Box 1147, Buckingham, PA 18912.

I.T. MANAGER BOOTCAMP IN A BOX™

A comprehensive step-by-step training program designed to help new I.T. Managers make the right career choices and gain the skills necessary for peak performance

For human resource professionals, performance consultants, and trainers in need of an easy to use and highly effective plug and play program.

The new IT Manager Bootcamp in a Box™, consists of approximately fifteen hours of development training, from orientation through the introduction to basic management skills. IT Manager Bootcamp in a Box™ was developed in conjunction with the critically acclaimed Manage I.T. book.

IT Manager Bootcamp in a Box™ was created to address the growing need for high performing IT managers and to facilitate rapid on-boarding of new IT managers. The training, designed to be delivered by in-house personnel, consists of the following:

New manager role orientation program

New manager skill orientation
- How to get the big picture and align yourself and your new team to it.
- Developing and using hiring plans.
- Getting to know your people.
- Giving feedback and conflict resolution.
- How to buy IT products and services.
- How to empower people and maintain stress control.
- How to benefit from outsourcing.

The IT Manager Bootcamp in a Box™ package includes:

- Leaders Guide — A step-by-step guide to enable rapid ramp-up to training.
- 10 copies of Manage I.T. paperback book.
- 10 Sets of Participant Materials.
- Participant's Certificate of Completion.
- Detailed PowerPoint presentations for each module.
- Leaders CD providing an audio overview of the program.
- Coaching Progress Journal*

* **Option:** The *IT Manager Bootcamp in a Box™* training can be followed-up with 6–12 weeks of in-person or telephone based individual and/or group coaching sessions, to reinforce application of the skills by the participant(s).

** If needed, qualified trainers can be provided to deliver the program as a supplement to your training staff.

Total Price $597.00 (US)

To order with a company purchase order or for more information, email jim@manageitbook.com or call (215) 794-3826

Our Guarantee — Your satisfaction with
IT Manager Bootcamp in a Box™ is fully guaranteed.

NOTES

NOTES

NOTES

NOTES

NOTES